Conducting Group Therapy with Addicts

A Guidebook for Professionals

Conducting Group Therapy with Addicts

A Guidebook for Professionals

Ivan R.
Elder, Ph.D.

Human Services Institute
Bradenton, Florida

TAB BOOKS
Blue Ridge Summit, PA

Library of Congress Cataloging-in-Publication Data

Elder, Ivan R.
    Conducting group therapy with addicts : a guidebook for professionals / by Ivan R. Elder.
        p. cm.
    ISBN 0-8306-3546-7X
    1. Substance abuse—Treatment 2. Group psychotherapy.
I. Title.
RC564.E43 1990
616.86'0651—dc20   89-20564
                                                         CIP

TAB BOOKS offers software for sale. For information and a catalog, please contact TAB Software Department, Blue Ridge Summit, PA 17294-0850.

Questions regarding the content of this book should be addressed to:

    Human Services Institute, Inc.
    P.O. Box 14610
    Bradenton, FL 34280

Development Editor: Lee Marvin Joiner, Ph.D.
Copy Editors: Pat Hammond and Mariette Petitpas

Contents

Preface

$\mathbf{A}$s a clinical psychologist, I have spent over fifteen years conducting group psychotherapy with addicts and supervising other therapists. This has given me a chance to learn about the nature of addiction from both a theoretical and a practical perspective and has offered me an opportunity to try different models, principles, and techniques. As a result, over the years, my colleagues and I have developed what I term the "Friendly Forces" model, an approach which embodies what addicts need most: powerful but supportive group confrontation of the addict's most basic problem—denial.

Effective group psychotherapy doesn't just happen in the clinical setting. Therapy must be planned and managed using a structure which guides both clients and therapists toward the therapeutic goal of overcoming the clients' denial. As a clinical psychologist, I have had the privilege of training psychiatry residents, social work interns, psychology interns, nursing students, medical students, addiction counselors, family practitioners, and a host of other allied health and mental health professionals in how to conduct group psychotherapy. I have seen firsthand what an intimidating experience this is for many of these students and how the anxiety they develop leads to confusion, excessively authoritarian management of the group, and other maladaptive strategies. Instead of promoting the group cohesion and force required to overcome denial, these tactics actually deplete and fragment group power. Students have often asked me for texts, books, or other sources of written documentation about my Friendly Forces model and so I decided to write *Conducting Group Therapy with Addicts*.

A student or mental health professional who reads and applies the principles outlined in this book will be able to conduct effective group psychotherapy for addicts from beginning to end, with little anxiety or difficulty. Although I do not recommend this as the *only* training necessary to conduct effective group psychotherapy, the book provides an extremely practical "how to" approach. The uniqueness of this book is that it both explains and illustrates the *process of empowering* group psychotherapy. Most important, the book will suggest practical solutions to commonly occurring problems in group therapy with addicts.

Conducting Group Therapy With Addicts addresses four main topics: 1) the nature of addiction, and why group psychotherapy is uniquely suited to helping an addict achieve greater self-knowledge and internal control; 2) how to conduct and empower group psychotherapy step by step, from forming and orienting the group to completing psychotherapy; 3) direct, practical strategies for dealing with common problems that occur during ongoing therapy and threaten to deplete its power; and 4) how you, as a therapist, can take practical steps to stay healthy psychologically and contribute maximally to the group process. The book contains numerous real examples of how addicts respond to problems, group processes in action, obstacles to group effectiveness, and therapists' responses to group problems and processes. It provides illustrations of "hands on" techniques therapists use in directing group psychotherapy.

The main theme of this book is how to *empower* the group to deal with the addict's denial, because it is the group, not the therapist, that has the potential force to overcome it. To maintain the focus on empowering the group to confront the addict's denial, I had to forgo a discussion of other ideas, practices, and techniques which are equally important to group psychotherapy. For example, I have not discussed the individual treatment of addicts who are in group psychotherapy, or the interface of different theoretical orientations, such as rational-emotive therapy or transactional analysis, with the Friendly Forces model.

One further word about the gender of pronouns used in this work. I have chosen to use the masculine or traditionally used gender forms he, his, him, and himself to represent both the masculine and feminine case. Such usage avoids what are undoubtedly more accurate, but also very awkward, dual-gender forms like his/her or s/he. I hope this will be acceptable to the reader.

Acknowledgments

I gratefully acknowledge the help, assistance, and intellectual stimulation of all the colleagues I have worked closely with over the years, particularly Mr. Kenneth Beard, Mrs. Glenna Brett, Mr. George Christian, Mr. Leo Glenn, Dr. Pete LeTang, and Dr. Carlos Ramirez at the VA Hospital in Tuscaloosa, Alabama; Dr. Al Acevedo, Mr. Charles Dawson, Mr. Scott Frederick, Mr. Andrew Harrison, Mrs. Mary Pickens, Dr. Praxedes Sebastian, and Mrs. Jean Young at the Dorn VA Hospital in Columbia, South Carolina. Mrs. Alma B. Greer deserves a special acknowledgment for her encouragement and many insights concerning interpersonal dynamics. All of these highly professional associates have taught me a great deal about group psychotherapy (and life, for that matter), either through direct observations or conversations we have had over the years.

I am also grateful to my family, particularly my wife Gail, for the warm support and time they have given this project. I remain deeply appreciative of Dr. Paul S. Siegel who inspired me to learn about the "headbone." I also remain deeply appreciative of Dr. Buford C. Arnold, whose early teachings provided such a solid basis for my later education.

Finally, I am very grateful for the very supportive and professional guidance I have received from my editor, Dr. Lee Joiner; unless one has been in the position of struggling to publish a book, one cannot understand the inestimable value of a knowledgeable and professional editor who champions your cause.

Addiction
DIAGNOSIS AND TREATMENT

One of the most troubling things about addiction is that unlike many illnesses, it hurts others besides the one who is sick. The people who are directly involved with the addict, his family and friends, and indirectly the entire society, are profoundly damaged, sometimes to an extent exceeding the effects upon the addict himself. There is literally no escape from addiction; the drug culture, disease, and crime which develop around drug addiction extend into all areas of our society.

You are undoubtedly aware of the great difficulty our nation faces in trying to treat drug and alcohol addiction effectively. Many of you have seen or felt the absolute devastation which addiction brings to the addict, his friends, and his loved ones. You may have watched addiction's destructive effects upon a drug user you have known or worked with: his loss of self-esteem, loss of personal control, and the life-threatening consequences to his health. Why do addicts persist in their course of self-destruction?

The key to understanding addiction is to understand the incredible power of the addict's denial, a condition which demands that it be countered with an extremely powerful treatment to combat the denial and the aberrant behavior it fosters. Group psychotherapy offers us that treatment power by virtue of the fact that even informal groups of people are influential change agents.

It takes only a little reflection to realize how forceful groups are, even in minor aspects of our lives. Consider, for instance, how uncomfortable you would be if you dressed inappropriately for work. Your "group" of co-workers would put tremendous pressure upon you to adopt appropriate dress even though they are not formally organized as a group with this particular function. Or consider one of the foremost anxiety-arousing situations: public speaking. Again, it is the expected evaluation of a "group" which carries such emotional potency. Imagine what a powerful force a group could be if we *organized and concentrated* it for the purpose of breaking through an addict's denial.

DIAGNOSING ADDICTION

Diagnosis is the first step in the treatment of addiction. Diagnosis is basically an effort to determine whether or not an individual is indeed addicted and requires treatment. Alcoholics Anonymous (A.A.) offered the first systematic approach to diagnosing and treating alcohol addiction or "alcoholism." In A.A. the diagnosis of alcoholism depends on the actions of the person himself—the "client." If someone goes to an A.A. meeting and declares a *desire* to stop drinking, he is accepted (diagnosed) as a genuine alcoholic. This self-declaration of a desire to stop drinking is the only prerequisite for membership in A.A.

As A.A. evolved, the Twelve Steps were formulated as a "treatment" for alcoholism. The Twelve Steps represented a summary of what the early A.A. members did to stay sober, forming a guideline for future alcoholics seeking sobriety. The A.A. movement also developed the Twelve Traditions. These traditions govern the conduct of A.A. groups, particularly in regard to their relationship with the outside or public world (Alcoholics Anonymous World Services, Inc. 1976).

Few of the diagnostic procedures we use today in alcohol and drug treatment centers are mentioned in the Alcoholics Anonymous program. Nothing in A.A. requires that the applicant demonstrate tolerance, withdrawal, or social/psychological impairments, to mention a few prominent clinical assessment concepts. The A.A. assessment is simple: the individual makes it himself. He goes to an A.A. meeting and embraces Step Number 1: "We admitted we were powerless over alcohol—that our lives had become unmanageable." He then follows the A.A. treatment which consists of attending A.A. meetings, working the Twelve Steps, following the Twelve Traditions, and, as "The Big Book" (A.A. members' fond nickname for their handbook *Alcoholics Anonymous*) suggests, doing anything else necessary and reasonable to stay sober.

The diagnosis of addiction is markedly different in a medical treatment center. If we are working in a medical establishment and seeking a diagnosis which meets insurers' reimbursement standards, we will probably use the medical diagnostic criteria in the *Diagnostic and Statistical Manual of Mental Disorders III - Revised* (better known as *DSM-III-R*). This manual requires that the diagnosis of alcohol or drug addiction (termed *Psychoactive Substance*

Dependence) meet two criteria. In brief, three of nine behavioral symptoms must have persisted for at least one month or have recurred over a long period of time. These diagnostic symptoms involve: loss of control over the use of the substance; a preoccupation with getting and using the substance, frequently to the point of intoxication; the disruption of social, occupational, and family life; continued use despite persistent adverse effects; the development of a tolerance and the need for increased doses; and, withdrawl symptoms and the taking of the substance to relieve them (American Psychiatric Association 1987).

Other attempts at identifying alcohol/drug addiction include researchers who have tried to define alcoholism and other drug addictions in terms of quantity and frequency indices of alcohol use combined with specific symptoms. Some researchers have defined alcoholism as consuming more than 3 ounces of absolute alcohol per day on the average or consuming more than 5 ounces on any one day, along with showing other symptoms such as "blackouts," "morning shakes," or "terminating eating" (Armor, Polich and Stambul 1978). Other investigators have defined alcoholism as consuming relatively large quantities of the drug, *with apparent loss of control*, such that one suffers serious problems and disabilities in: 1) social functioning, e.g., divorce, firings from jobs, avoidance by former friends; 2) psychological functioning, e.g., lowered self-esteem, depression, guilt, anxiety, etc.; and 3) medical/health, e.g., cirrhosis, pancreatitis, organic brain dysfunction, heart dysfunction, or delirium tremens (Barry 1974).

Although there is no universal set of criteria which will unfailingly diagnose every addict to the satisfaction of all professionals, we still find a great deal of agreement among different professionals assessing a single case.

Despite the emphasis on scientific diagnosis and standardization, I think most professionals would be glad to treat anyone who sincerely labeled himself an "addict" and could provide some supporting evidence, even though the facts might not be entirely consistent with the "standard" criteria. So, labels and diagnoses are best considered *flexible guidelines* for determining who needs treatment.

When we diagnose addiction in the wake of overwhelming evidence of addiction, it is unnecessary that a client agree with the diagnosis. Even though A.A. emphasizes self-definition of addiction as a basis for treatment, an alcoholic or drug addict is not the only person who can label himself as such, any more than someone with lung cancer is the final arbiter of a diagnosis of disease pathology. It is certainly preferable that the addict agree with an accurate diagnosis of addiction because this means he has broken through denial and probably will be more motivated to cooperate fully in the treatment program.

Although therapists might ideally prefer to work with clients who have recognized their own addiction, many clients remain highly resistant to the diagnosis even though they realize that something is "dead wrong." When the facts are more ambiguous, and it becomes difficult to tell whether the person presenting for treatment is indeed an addict, then his own opinion about his condition carries more weight in the diagnosis. In the case of either ambiguous facts or highly resistant addicts, family members should be consulted. Besides adding their personal insights, family members may be able to corroborate addictive behavior patterns noted in the clinical diagnosis.

While diagnosis seeks to answer the question: "Is this person addicted?", the act of diagnosis and the information which is gained from it invariably lead to treatment recommendations. These treatment recommendations stem from some conceptual model that represents our ideas about the origin or cause of the addiction and its appropriate treatment. Sometimes the models which guide our work are visible, prominent, and explicit such as the Twelve Steps. But often our models are implicit and not so clearly spelled out.

TREATMENT MODELS

A.A.'s founders perceived alcoholism as an "allergy" to alcohol, a response which ultimately accounted for the addiction. It is the alcoholic's obsession to drink normally. He continually attempts to drink to relax, as many people do, but with a highly negative, self-destructive outcome. Still, the alcoholic persists, even when the harmful outcomes of his drinking are clear to everyone —except perhaps to himself. This obsession to drink normally accounts for the chronicity of alcoholism and the relapse to drinking which often follows treatment (Alcoholics Anonymous World Services, Inc. 1976).

The A.A. treatment involves abstaining from alcohol, attending A.A. meetings regularly, and following the Twelve Steps ("Step-work"), in order to overcome addiction to the point of being "recovering." (According to the A.A. program, one never is cured of alcoholism. One is always trying to recover from the effects of alcoholism and to avoid a relapse.) The A.A. treatment is psychosocial in that much of its impact occurs through a social medium— A.A. meetings. It is also an individualized program. A.A. members make a careful self-examination of their own personal lives and values (Alcoholics Anonynmous World Services, Inc. 1976).

"The Big Book" recommends seeking any reasonable treatment that is likely to prevent the alcoholic's further addiction. As addiction treatment has become "medicalized," "psychologized," "sociologized," and "counselorized," we have adopted alternative strategies of labeling and diagnosis, each of which connote a particular conceptual model and assumptions about treatment. For example, calling alcoholism a disease immediately puts the problem into the medical realm. Once the problem is "medicalized," a physician becomes the appropriate person to consult for help and a medical establishment becomes the appropriate locus for treatment.

Psychologists, on the other hand, might call addiction a behavior disorder, notwithstanding the necessary admission that the sequelae of alcoholic bouts (e.g., cirrhosis) need medical attention. Sociologists or social workers might describe addiction in social terms. In fact, some sociological theorists argue that alcoholism is a social-systems problem. They argue that to focus on the addict alone, and to see him as the problem, is to "scapegoat" the addict and lose the appropriate focus of treatment—the family, local community, and, by extension, the whole continuum of social systems throughout the entire culture.

Sometimes our diagnosis and treatment models tell us more about the treatment agent than the addict or his condition. For example, if we were to take the extreme position that the addict has a narrowly defined disease, then we might search for a virus or germ, just as we would look for streptococci in the case of a sore throat. In the medical model, we would emphasize the usual medical treatments—surgery, medications, rest and recuperation.

Similarly, if we took a very narrowly focused psychological approach, we would assume that the entire problem of addiction lay within the psyche; thus, psychotherapy would be the paramount and only treatment for addiction.

Comparably, if we were to take the extreme sociological position, that alcoholism is a symptom of a system problem, then we would concern ourselves with the alcoholic's family and significant others, possibly seeing direct treatment of the alcoholic as secondary. We would not treat the alcoholic without attempting to alter the social context of his disorder. In the most extreme of these sociological models, we would concentrate our efforts on the political system because it guides the interaction of social systems. Every health problem would be a political problem requiring a political treatment or solution.

REPEATED CHOICES

The Friendly Forces model for group therapy described in this book is based on the premise that addictions are not "caused" by anything other than the *repeated choice* to use an addictive substance to the point of addiction. These choices are encouraged by genetic, psychological and social conditions which work together or *interact*.

Let's consider an example of this approach. A young man, Mr. Smith, has a history of alcoholism in his family. His father and grandfather were both alcoholics, suggesting a strong *genetic factor*. Mr. Smith also has a very passive-aggressive or antisocial personality and frequently expresses strong feelings of anger and resentment. He fails to resolve these feelings and is chronically agitated. His inability to resolve his negative feelings and inner conflicts represents a *psychological factor* in his addiction. Suppose Mr. Smith marries a woman who encourages or enables his drinking. When Mr. Smith drinks too much on the weekend, she calls the boss and tells him her husband is "sick" and will be absent from work. Moreover, suppose Mr. Smith's close friends are heavy drinkers who see heavy drinking as an appropriate means of coping with life's problems. Both the wife and friends would represent a strong *social factor*, supporting and encouraging the choice of heavy drinking.

A very important premise of the Friendly Forces model is that one's choices are essentially free, not determined absolutely by either the outer or inner environment but *strongly encouraged by such forces*. In the example above, genetic, psychological, and social factors strongly encourage the choice to drink heavily and to continue drinking unabated in spite of negative outcomes. These multiple factors increase the odds of choosing to drink heavily, but one can still choose to abstain, although this will require some effort and perhaps maladjustment. In the field of alcoholism treatment, such abstainers are referred to as "dry drunks." They have all the dynamics which produce an alcoholic and yet they don't drink. However, let's suppose that Mr. Smith responds in accordance with the probabilities and continues to drink heavily. This is where the interactive nature of the factors begins to develop.

As Mr. Smith drinks more and more, he will probably begin to cling to a social group supportive of that behavior, spending more and more time with drinking buddies, who in turn continue to encourage increased drinking. This group buffers him against healthier forces which might discourage drinking ("Hey, man, don't let your wife run your life, stay a little longer and let's have a few more drinks"). The social factors support the choice of drinking and the drinking strengthens the social set. This is just one of many social factor interactions which fuel the addiction.

Another interaction occurs when the communication between Mr. Smith and his wife continues to deteriorate and he becomes more and more unhappy in his marriage. His deepening marital despair encourages him to drink more, which further deteriorates and aggravates his already shaky marriage.

As a passive-aggressive personality, Mr. Smith tends to suppress his anger, becoming brooding and resentful. He may use alcohol to smother and deny these emotions temporarily. His alcoholic bouts offer him the opportunity to act out and discharge his anger and resentment at a time when he isn't conscious of what he is doing, thereby providing some emotional catharsis or "relief." We see how a pattern emerges here which is bigger and more complex than the simple sum of its parts. The more Mr. Smith drinks to handle his emotions, the more emotional problems develop. Drinking does not solve the emotional problems he is denying and avoiding; it merely masks them for the moment, allowing him brief catharsis. Then drinking compounds the emotional distress with new problems, such as missing more and more work, being fired, or abusing his wife or children. Now he has new worries, guilt, and anxiety. And he still has his original problem of chronic anger and resentment.

The social and psychological factors and their respective cycles of increasing motivation for addiction interact strongly with the genetic tendency toward addiction and with each other. For example, as the addict becomes increasingly involved in his addiction, he loses self-esteem and self-confidence. This loss of self-esteem and self-confidence affects his relations with others. He may feel so guilty that he unconsciously plans ways to make his wife leave him as a punishment for his guilt. If his wife leaves him, he suffers a further drop in self-esteem.

If life was simple, and causes and effects were singular in their influence, simplistic models of cause and effect might be useful. By carefully studying addiction, we might arrive at some theorem such as: A causes B, B causes C, C causes addiction. However, the true complexity of the world is such that A, B, and C all have some connection with addiction and they all *interact with each other and addiction*. In other words, A affects B, B affects A, C affects B, B affects C, A affects C, C affects A, and addiction interacts with all of these variables.

Many popular models of addiction suggest just the opposite. They are inherently simple one-directional cause-and-effect models. Extremely simplistic models, such as the idea that drinking causes all the psychological problems you see in an alcoholic (Beardslee and Vaillant 1984), suggest that a psychologically healthy person somehow uses or drinks in a very unhealthy fashion. Williams (1976) noted that the reverse position has also been put forward: that all alcoholics or addicts share the same personality configuration. The implicit assumption is that this special personality "causes" the addiction. But personality assessments have shown that there is no one "addictive" personality, pointing out the inadequacy of such simplistic notions of cause-and-effect. The world is a much more complicated system than a simple cause-and-effect model can accommodate.

Another example of this simplistic thinking is the notion that all addiction is reducible to just *one factor*—genetic, sociological or psychological. Many alcoholics entering treatment feel that their alcoholism is genetic and that their emotions have nothing to do with developing or maintaining alcoholism. This model ignores the multitude of choices humans make daily which greatly affect whether they ultimately become addicted to substances. I recently heard an authority in the field of alcoholism profess that he was not responsible for his alcoholism; it was a genetic problem. This is stunning in view of the fact that he described a drinking history of over a dozen years during which he repeatedly made the choice to continue using alcohol despite negative consequences. This is equivalent to saying that the genetic makeup of the person caused him to make such repeated choices, something that most of us would consider highly unlikely.

Yes, we see genetics directly shape the behavior of babies who suck instinctively at the nipple. But this is a far cry from saying that genetics alone is causing one to make repeated choices to use alcohol as an adult. Moreover, this is the same adult who makes highly discriminating choices in the rest of his environment. He may be a brain surgeon who is highly skilled and well-known in his field, making highly discriminating choices based upon psychological and social motivations. Yet, we are asked to believe that he is responding to alcohol simply on the basis of genetics. This genetic argument also ignores the whole field of abnormal psychology, which routinely shows that, given a genetic predisposition for almost any abnormality or disorder, the most likely outcome is *nonoccurrence of the disorder* (Carson, Butcher and Coleman 1988).

Many alcoholics and drug addicts express other over-simplifications upon entering treatment. For example, an alcoholic client may say that he drinks only "because of the taste," or "out of habit" and this produced his alcoholism. Again, it is as if taste or habit removed the choice, with all its psychological and social motivations, and this one cause, totally divorced from any characteristics of any other variable in nature, produced this one effect: addiction. Then this one effect itself became a cause and produced all the addict's social and psychological problems. When we think logically about this, we realize that such notions don't come close to mirroring the true complexity of life.

Psychological and social problems usually are the result of complex circumstances involving several events and factors which combine or interact. Interacting factors in addiction can best be examined by comparing addiction with other multifactorial diseases. For example, we all know that heart disease is a condition resulting from the interactions of many different factors. There is a hereditary component. If your father or mother died of a heart attack, it increases the probability that you will. There are sociological factors involved. Your culture may encourage a high-fat diet, encourage high-stress activities, or encourage habits which are harmful to the cardiovascular system, such as smoking. There is also a psychological factor, such as your effort to resist, or your surrender to, Type A behavior. There are self-esteem issues which determine whether you will seek medical care for health maintenance, and whether you will develop self-discipline enough to maintain a healthy diet and exercise level.

If we were to apply some of the simplistic addiction models to heart disease, we would draw incorrect conclusions. Smoking would invariably produce heart attacks and death. Type A behaviors would invariably result in death by heart attack. Anyone who ate a high-fat diet would die of a stroke or heart disease.

An interactive model suggests that, as you increase the number of heart disease factors present in your life, the probability increases that you will develop heart disease. If you smoke three packs of cigarettes a day, eat saturated fats, live a "high-voltage" life, never exercise, and your father and mother both died of heart attacks, then the probability is high that you also will develop heart disease. Notice that these factors interact with each other.

It is not unusual for a person who is a high-stress or Type A personality to smoke to relax. One who is overweight and eating a nutritionally inadequate diet may avoid exercising because it is experienced as too exhausting for someone so heavy. The person whose self-esteem is low may begin to develop symptoms of heart disease but feel "helpless" to do anything about them; his smoking may increase due to nervousness about his symptoms.

What are the treatments which an interactive model suggests? In the case of heart disease, the physician encourages the client to make a commitment to act in favor of a healthy heart. Then the physician recommends that the client decrease his cholesterol level, stop smoking, exercise more, and learn to relax. These positive changes may in themselves produce other positive changes. For example, if a client starts to exercise, he may also try to stop smoking because physical fitness begins to feel good and worthwhile. Smoking would be seen as undermining this and might produce "cognitive dissonance."

This is extremely similar to the process of recovery in the addict! We encourage the addict to make the choice of refraining from further drug or alcohol use, without which other changes are impossible. Then, we encourage the addict to work on social factors which may be increasing the likelihood of making that choice. We tell him to "change playgrounds and playmates" or to find new acquaintances at A.A./N.A. He should refrain from prolonged contact with old "using" buddies. The addict should encourage his spouse to become involved in Al-Anon or Nar-Anon so that any codependent patterns can be disrupted. Family therapy may also be used to confront any marital and family discord which might encourage the addictive choice.

We also encourage the addict to make psychological changes. Slogans like "Easy Does It" and treatments like relaxation therapy both combat Type A behavior. "Don't get hungry, angry, lonely or tired" and "stress management" advise the addict to avoid "high-drive" or emotionally laden states that make him prone to impulsive behavior. Group or individual psychotherapy may be employed to help bring about change in self-destructive lifestyles. Again, we see positive changes in all the addiction-supporting factors when one of them begins to change. When the addict begins to recover, his self-esteem begins to improve, which allows him to develop more self-discipline. This enables him to begin to reduce his Type A behavior. This in turn boosts his self-esteem higher still.

The net result is that by reducing the strength of critical psychological and social factors *the addict sharply lowers the probability that he will be motivated to make the addictive choice*. It becomes easier and more satisfying to choose sobriety. But notice a tremendous caveat: even though we reduce the strength of these contributing factors, the addict can still make the addictive choice. It is not these factors themselves, but rather the person's choice to use addictive substances that counts.

2

The Addict
INNER AND OUTER REALITIES

If we can decrease the effects of the social and psychological factors which support and encourage addiction, we lessen the chance that the addict will again make the addictive choice. Providing a means of achieving this is one of the important contributions of group psychotherapy to recovery. But before discussing how group therapy accomplishes this important result, we must examine certain features of the addict's personality which have affected his development and which affect how he responds to therapy.

As we develop, we all experience the interplay of "outer" and "inner" factors in our continuing struggle to adapt. "Outer" factors are those events and forces which occur outside of ourselves, but which nevertheless have a strong impact upon us. Outer factors include other people, their actions toward us, and the material world. The crucial outer factors of childhood are our parents or parental substitutes—how they treated us, reinforced us, reacted to us and our achievement or failure to achieve; and whether they were cold, loving, critical, unapproving, harsh, abusive, or doting. Another powerful outer factor which shapes our development is the general culture we grew up in—from the local sociocultural environment right up to the national scene in which we developed. Someone growing up in the Great Depression, for instance, would have markedly different outer factors to cope with than someone who grew up in the late 1960's.

"Inner" factors include such things as our self-concept, how we think about ourselves in relation to others, and if, in fact, we think about ourselves at all. Inner factors also include our dispositions and our inherited traits of personality: for instance, whether we are prone to be worriers, have temper tantrums, or have low versus high energy levels. One decisive inner factor is self-knowledge, the ability to be aware of what is happening to us internally and to take appropriate action to relieve our inner tensions. For example, if I am angry or depressed, I cannot begin to feel good until I am willing to recognize my anger and consider what I might be contributing to its maintenance.

The well-adjusted person is attuned to both outer and inner factors in his life, but a major trauma can skew this balance. One of the most serious reactions to traumatic outer factors is the shifting of attention from one's "inner" life to the "outer" world. Frequently, the addict has suffered from a traumatic outer event such as the death of a parent at an early age, the divorce or repeated divorce of a parent, or extremely abusive parents. A preoccupation with outer factors may occur, for example, when a 12-year-old boy's father dies and he is overwhelmed by a trauma he is not emotionally equipped to handle. He may feel forced to assume the father's role, shelving his inner development in order to deal with an overwhelming outer reality. Such people divert their energies increasingly into the outer, external world and less and less into their inner subjective world of feelings, thoughts, and perceptions. We would say they had developed an excess of "outsight" at a cost of reduced "insight." This development leaves them with sharply decreased adaptive abilities and also begins to shape the whole course of their future development. We can see the negative effects of shifting attention primarily to the outer world if we take a moment to look at stress and adaptation.

Stress = **Interaction** of Inner and Outer Factors
Adaptation = **Interaction** of Inner and Outer Factors

If, for example, Mr. Smith and Mr. Johnson both lose their jobs, Mr. Smith, who is a tense worrier, will undoubtedly experience more stress than Mr. Johnson, who is more confident under the same circumstances. Both experience a stressful outer event (job loss), but Mr. Smith's inner factors (heightened tension and worry) will interact with and intensify the stress potential of the outer events.

Mr. Smith may certainly improve his adaptation by either improving his self-confidence (lowering his anxiety and tension) or by obtaining another job—or by both. The "Serenity Prayer" could be construed as showing how we can use both inner and outer factors to achieve serenity:

God grant me the serenity to accept the things I cannot change, the courage to change the things I can, and the wisdom to know the difference.

For the addict, there may not be anything which he feels he cannot change. Further, notice that to accept the things we cannot change requires the ability to do "inner work" wherein we talk to ourselves about being "limited," "human," and "finite," and humble ourselves to these realities. Limitations force the rational person to reflect upon his nature and to accept it rather than to "beat one's head against the [immutable] wall." Note, however, that the adolescent in our previous example has lost some adaptive capability: he has shifted so much attention to outer factors (outsight) that he has lost the capacity to use inner change (insight). For him, stress is external, and so is adaptation—thus, our formulas for him would read:

$$\text{Stress} = \text{Result of } \textit{Outer} \text{ Factors}$$
$$\text{Adaptation} = \text{Change in } \textit{Outer} \text{ Factors}$$

This person sees "adjustment" as being on the outside, in external factors. If there are problems in this person's marriage, they are perceived as completely the spouse's responsibility. The spouse must therefore do all the changing. Although the wife may be causing the husband trouble, it is, to be sure, not one hundred percent of the trouble. His reaction to the problem, from the perspective of other people, is to become demanding. Others are the ones who are expected to change completely, although if confronted he may deny feeling this way.

It is no coincidence that our future addict becomes "controlling" and "obsessed with power and manipulation." His only means of adjustment has become one of changing the external world, and he must have power and control in order to do so. Naturally enough, the other people in this person's life do not completely consent to his demands without a fight. Their reluctance to accept blame and cooperate with his schemes enrages him. Their unwillingness to consent to his manipulations makes him feel unfairly treated. When others refuse to do his bidding, the future addict starts blaming others, feeling that everything which goes wrong is everyone else's fault. His *incorrect* personal formula takes over: Stress = Result of Outer Factors. His blaming intensifies his anger, and these strong inner feelings become even more troubling because he does not know how to deal with inner stresses. So, he immediately begins to try to rid himself of inner stresses by striving to push inner problems to the outside.

DENIAL

First the addict denies. He tells himself he simply isn't angry and doesn't feel bad. He maintains this even though his face may be beet-red and he may be clenching his fist while he talks about his wife or children. Others who see his apparent emotional distress may be aghast that he is denying his anger and may even accuse him of lying. Anyone who has ever worked with addicts will attest that the denial of feelings of any kind is often astounding to the observer. Not only does the addict deny troublesome feelings, he denies feelings in general. In short, his denial of inner feeling states can be just as strong and total as his initial denial of addiction. Confrontation will be required to help break through this denial.

ACTING OUT

Second, the addict tends to solve problems of inner stress by acting out, instead of using verbal/social problem-solving solutions. Acting out is defined here as taking quick, impulsive, poorly planned, physical action in the external environment. It is designed to quickly reduce the addict's current distress. For example, acting out might take the form of an angry employee walking off the job without notice. An unhappily married person might suddenly leave and obtain a hasty divorce. A person who has been insulted might hit someone in a fit of anger.

The advantage and attraction of acting out is that it reduces stress rapidly. In the short term, acting out relieves the addict of having to deal with or experience distressing inner realities. The disadvantage of acting out is that although it produces quick, short-term relief, eventually the stress returns with a vengeance. After repeatedly walking off jobs, a person will still have difficulty working with others. But now he also has a poor work history, which makes it more difficult to obtain new employment.

VERBAL/SOCIAL PROBLEM-SOLVING

Verbal/social problem-solving, in contrast to acting out, involves talking and reasoning with ourselves and others in order to reduce stress. Examples of this kind of problem-solving range from simply sharing emotional feelings with a friend or talking out problems with colleagues to more involved strategies such as formal psychotherapy. The disadvantage of these techniques is that they don't often yield immediate solutions. A serious marital problem can't be solved in a single counseling session. However, verbal/social problem-solving does lead to long term solutions that can permanently reduce stress. If a marital conflict is identified and a solution found, it is less likely to be a recurring problem in the future.

Verbal/social problem-solving brings to bear "friendly forces." This is the premise upon which our Friendly Forces model of group psychotherapy is based. We plan our responses to life's problems by inviting others who are important to us, or who we feel have greater knowledge about a problem than we do, to share their thoughts and opinions. This sharing broadens our perspective, clarifies our choices, and helps us to establish realistic goals.

For example, if I want to resolve a conflict with my superiors, I could "act out," rushing into their offices with abusive threats and demands. But this will not help me solve my problem permanently or achieve my long-range goals. A verbal/social problem-solving approach would require that I think about the goals I want to achieve, and the procedures I can use to achieve them. I might talk with colleagues, "pick their brains," and get their opinions about how to approach my problem and attain my goals. Some of these people may perceive problems and solutions which I am unable to see. They may be able to see flaws in my thinking which result from my being too close to the problem. This problem-solving approach eventually becomes a decision-by-consensus wherein "two (or more) *reasoning* heads are better than one."

The verbal/social problem-solving approach is uncomfortable for the addict since it requires patience and a willingness to experience and deal with disturbing inner realities without instant results. This is something the addict resists. Remember, the addict acts out to decrease inner distress immediately and refocus on the external or outside world.

SUBSTANCE ABUSE AS A FORM OF ACTING OUT

The addict may also act out with drugs and alcohol. Alcohol or drugs will alter his state of consciousness so that he can escape his inner feelings temporarily. Using alcohol or drugs as a coping strategy gets rid of disturbing inner experiences without the addict having to consciously struggle with them. Notice too that drugs and alcohol are slowly drawn into the web of "pushing everything to the outside." When alcohol or drugs become a problem, they too are denied. The addict proclaims,

I'm not an alcoholic (drug addict),

even though everyone around him may be utterly convinced that he's hopelessly addicted.

Even when the addict is willing to admit that he has some trouble, it is with reservations.

I can still control my drinking.

Finally, if he admits addiction, the addiction itself is pushed to the outside.

If I could only stop drinking, everything would be okay.

If I just lived on an island without drugs, I would have no problems.

My wife and I only have problems when I'm drinking.

I never miss work because of my cocaine—in fact, it bolsters my performance.

Such extreme statements reveal that this is a person who doesn't know himself. In terms of what I said earlier, he completely ignores the inner factors. He lacks the ability to recognize what is happening inside himself. Our addict has become almost the opposite of the ancient Greeks who counseled that the greatest wisdom comes from "knowing thyself."

His failure to control life, particularly his own, slowly begins to intrude upon his consciousness and causes a budding growth of self-hatred which eventually becomes quite strong. So, here is an individual who set out to control life and himself by "willpower," but who is thwarted at every turn. He slowly realizes that he is failing at everything and controlling nothing.

PREPARING TO DIE

Finally, there is the supreme negative consequence. Knowing nothing about himself and therefore unable to care about himself, he proceeds to systematically kill himself with drugs or alcohol. This, too, he denies. This is a shocking conclusion, but one I believe is valid. We see it regularly in treatment centers and in the everyday world of "lesser addictions" such as cigarette smoking. This is why medical sermons, about how an addict will die if he continues drinking or using, rarely work. Lacking genuine self-knowledge, the addict is already unconsciously prepared to kill himself. And the more the addict loses control of himself and his life, the more he denies.

This is a typical psychological portrait of the man or woman who enters treatment for an addiction. Completely out of touch with his inner self, struggling to change the outer world through power and control, he uses denial, acting out, and alcohol and drugs to continue to avoid the inner realities. All problems have been forced to the outside.

You might be saying, "So what?" The point is that this individual has less than half his adaptive power working for him. He can adjust only by controlling or changing the outer world. In addition, he is a person who doesn't know himself and therefore can't really like or love himself; a person who, in fact, is filled with self-hate at his inability to control the outer world, perhaps even hating himself enough to want to kill himself. Imagine this person trying to "get better" or recover from addiction; not only does he not know anything about his inner problems which are driving the addiction, but also he can't "hear" when others try to tell him what the problem is. He uses denial and defensiveness when others focus on his own personal problems which are driving the addiction. He comes up, instead, with a superficial and external method of recovery, using "will power" to resist the urge to drink or use drugs. From this vantage point, it is no mystery that addiction tends to be a chronic disorder, which is overcome only after repeated relapses.

3

Why Group Psychotherapy?
THE FORCES OF CHANGE

Group psychotherapy is a unique and powerful form of structured social interaction through which an addict can learn how others view his attitudes, ideas, and feelings. It is a Friendly Force which moves the addict toward successful recovery by helping him gain sensitivity to his own inner reality and achieve greater self-knowledge, one cornerstone of a successful recovery.

As I indicated in Chapter Two, the most prominent characteristics of the addict are denial of inner problems and a preoccupation with external reality. Any professional working with addicts will confirm that addicted persons have great difficulty accepting that they have an addiction problem and consistently make choices which maintain it. This denial explains why so many addicted persons must suffer tremendous losses and expose themselves to physical diseases or violence before coming to the realization that they do indeed have a problem.

A physician, for example, becomes frustrated when the same alcoholic repeatedly comes to the emergency room after having been referred again and again for psychiatric help. But even when an addict undertakes treatment, denial may remain strong and lead to a relapse. Many addicted persons are rehabilitated, achieve six months' sobriety and then reinstate their addictions, in part because of the denial of their addiction. Friends, relatives, supervisors, and coworkers often see clearly the destructive effects of the addictive pattern and point this out to the addict. Still he denies his addiction and continues to pursue the addictive choice. It is the fact that the addicted person often uses massive denial to evade his addiction problem and avoid other emotional issues which prompts us to employ group psychotherapy.

THE IMPORTANCE OF FEEDBACK

Feedback is the reaction we get to our behavior. For example, if we are too aggressive the feedback we receive from others may be quite negative. The people toward whom we are aggressive may eventually avoid us completely. If we are charming and courteous, others will probably be pleased with us and seek out our company and companionship. However, in order for this feedback to register and have an effect on our later behavior, we must be open to it.

Someone with impaired hearing or vision has great difficulty receiving feedback from others because of sensory limitations. The addict is like a person with a sensory impairment, except that *his* feedback impairment is a function of his personality trait development. He doesn't really want feedback about himself because it would disturb his view of himself and the events in his life. Remember, he is intent on pushing everything to the "outside," making every internal problem of his own into an external problem of someone else. We speak to the addict, and yet he doesn't "hear."

The addict's spouse, physician, and friends are all astonished at his insensitivity to feedback. They repeatedly point out his self-destructiveness which, while so patently clear to them, simply does not register on his consciousness. Imagine the addict's resistance to a single professional talking face-to-face with him about his addictive choices. When a psychiatrist or psychologist gives the addict feedback in reaction to something he said or did, the addict immediately starts to discount it by thinking, "Boy, who does this guy think he is—why he probably doesn't even drink!"

Besides his denial, the addict has learned to be manipulative and "conning." He has learned how to tell people what they want to hear or what will satisfy them enough to get what he wants. Consider the following example.

[Dr. J.]: How much have you been drinking in the last week?

[Ms. K.]: [acting very intoxicated, slurred speech, unsteady posture, ruddy complexion]: Oh, just a few beers now and then, nothing excessive—you know, you come in from a hot day and then you just want a few beers and that's about it.

[Dr. J.]: But your husband says that you've gotten drunk quite a few times in the last week.

[Ms. K.]: Geez, Doc, don't you know nothing about men? He's been drinking a lot himself and is trying to make me look bad just because I like to have two or three beers when I come in. God, if he'd just mind his own business, I wouldn't have had to come here to be checked out.

Please, Doc, just let me go and I'll handle him and we won't be back to bother you.

If you haven't worked with addicts you might be misled by this manipulative behavior and the clear-cut lack of interest the addict showed for her husband and herself.

The addict uses all his defenses to block out feedback, including denial, rationalization, conning, manipulation, changing the subject, and obfuscation through long, confused answers to questions in an attempt to avoid "hearing" feedback about himself. In order to get through to the addict, to let him become aware of what is happening to him, and to help him recognize its seriousness, we must increase the intensity of the feedback. One way to do this is through group psychotherapy, a means of giving each group member prolonged, intensive, and very specific feedback about himself from all the other members of the group.

Group therapy can amplify feedback because a group can be organized to focus on one individual at a time. When one of the members "presents," the rest of the group focuses entirely upon that person and in so doing provides maximum feedback. Although it may be easy to shrug off one person's feedback (including a professional's), it is much more difficult to shrug off eleven other group members who back up their opinions with evidence from your daily living and interactions with them. Countless experiments show how group pressure can be extremely powerful in promoting behavior change.

Imagine yourself confronted by a group of twelve to fifteen peers about one of your personality or behavior characteristics. The pressure to thoroughly examine your problem would be intense. If group psychotherapy takes place in an inpatient setting, the feedback may be even more powerful. For one thing, the group members are living together and have twenty-four hours every day to observe each other and notice problematic behavior patterns. Remember, the addict is a very astute and insightful person when looking outside himself.

When a group in an inpatient program gives feedback to a "presenter," members typically have a great deal of evidence to back up their statements. One of the things we have learned through research is that the most persuasive arguments offer some type of evidence. When it comes to our own behavior, we are more persuaded when those giving us feedback include some concrete examples of our behavior:

[Ms. J.]: You know, I've been noticing that you're very demanding and you also lose your temper when you don't get your way with people.

[Mr. B.]: That's not true, and I resent the implication.

[Ms. J.]: But just think about it. This morning you stormed out of the cafeteria after throwing your tray on the floor because you couldn't get extra bacon. You also swore at the nurse the other day when she got you out of bed because you were late to the film session. You don't see other clients acting that way, do you?

[Mr. B.]: Well, maybe I do have quite a temper, but you know these people around here don't always treat us very well either.

The evidence was helpful in nudging our presenter just a little toward realizing that he himself causes some of the chronic anger and agitation he experiences. Progress is slow, however, and we cannot expect a complete realization that one is "demanding" in a single group session.

A further advantage of group therapy in an inpatient setting is that the feedback extends beyond the formal session of sixty to ninety minutes. If patients are coalescing into a good therapeutic group, they will probably continue to give the presenter feedback for the entire day, several days, or even weeks. This greatly intensifies the force of the therapy.

Although you might wonder how effective a group that consists entirely of members who are addicted can be, I have found that such groups work well. Because of their knowledge of how addicts think and behave, group members are fully aware of the defenses, manipulations, and denial patterns of addicts. They are "hard to fool."

Participating in group therapy offers additional benefits to the addicted person. The model I will describe later specifies that the group work *intensively* with one individual per session, but this individual is not the only one who benefits. If the group members are all active participants and honestly express their reactions, then they too will learn verbal/social problem-solving techniques such as reasoning and talking to regulate emotional concerns. Even for the member who is not presenting, group therapy provides a chance to examine feelings, express feelings assertively, confront difficult interpersonal situations, and learn the value of seeking others' opinions and perspectives. A very passive person who learns to give honest feedback to others in the group is learning to relate more to his own internal factors, too, increasing his adaptive ability and helping himself.

Many addicts become quite withdrawn and suffer tremendously from a sense of social isolation, of being "different." The addict begins to believe that he is the only one in the world with problems, and this produces intense feelings of alienation and estrangement. He feels cut off from the human race. The ensuing depression and loneliness inspire further addiction. However, when this person participates in group therapy, the sharing of emotions brings about the development of intimacy and a sense of belonging. The group members' renewed ability to form relationships, to be able to ventilate emotions and to know that they are indeed not "freaks" or "subhuman monsters" bolsters self-esteem and builds confidence.

As addicts in group therapy learn to become assertive and develop greater feelings of intimacy, they practice important behaviors which transfer to the real world environment. Essentially, they learn how to relate to others in a healthy fashion, how to share emotions, and how to develop a sense of belonging with others with whom they live.

In summary, the following features of this group therapy model make it optimum for treating the addict:

- Each session focuses entirely on one person, and the entire group provides powerful feedback to help break through his denial and defensiveness.

- By including only addicts, the group is not vulnerable to any single member's attempts at denial, conning, manipulation, and obfuscation.

- If the group coalesces into a healthy, close-knit group, then the power of the therapy in an inpatient setting will be extended through the continuous daily interaction of members.

- By giving feedback to others and talking about emotions, group members practice verbal/social problem-solving methods which will help them to cope with life after discharge.

- By encouraging commonality and belonging, the group provides a chance to demonstrate and foster healthy relationships.

4

Getting Started
AN ENVIRONMENT FOR CHANGE

The Friendly Forces model is appropriate for the addict who is fairly intact, psychologically and organically. While we expect addicts to have personality problems, the approach described in this book is best suited for the client who is nonpsychotic, with no gross impairment in his ability to perceive reality. The primary reason for this is that a psychotic client might experience auditory and visual hallucinations, creating a markedly different perceptual world for him. If this occurs, he will have great difficulty developing a relationship with other group members.

There are other drawbacks to mixing psychotic clients with nonpsychotic clients. Psychotic clients are grossly impaired in their ability to both give and receive honest feedback. Earlier I described the addict as one who has great "outsight," but very poor insight. In that instance, I was referring to the nonpsychotic addict. The psychotic addict has gross disturbances in his ability to assess realistically the behaviors of others and to give them useful feedback. For example, let's consider what might happen with a paranoid schizophrenic in a group in which he is the only psychotic. During a presentation, the paranoid schizophrenic might start having delusions that the presenter is an FBI agent who is after him and trying to poison him. Such gross perceptual distortions render the schizophrenic's feedback totally meaningless. Furthermore, when the schizophrenic begins to utter bizarre feedback the other group members may begin to scapegoat and reject him. Worse still, when the schizophrenic presents and the group is urged to give him honest, confronting feedback, they may say, "You're crazy." I have in fact witnessed this in experimental groups before. Such feedback cannot be healthy when one considers the vulnerability of the schizophrenic client.

In addition, the Friendly Forces model works best if the client is not more than mildly organically impaired. Here I am referring to brain dysfunction or brain damage. It probably will be difficult for the organically impaired client, in a group of intact clients, to accurately assess the presenter and his situation. This problem stems from his impairment in short-term memory and conceptual or abstract thinking. When receiving feedback himself, the client with organic brain dysfunction may have great difficulty understanding the sometimes abstract thoughts of other group members. Nevertheless, it must be said that, in general, even the moderately brain-damaged client can prosper better in the group than the psychotic client can. One reason is that most groups tend to feel sympathy for the moderately brain-damaged client.

The Friendly Forces model can easily handle clients with other types of dual diagnoses. Two examples of dual diagnoses commonly encountered in treatment facilities are alcoholism plus antisocial personality and drug dependence plus borderline personality. The key to productive group psychotherapy for the dual diagnosis client is good reality contact—perceiving and thinking like most other people. Although the antisocial and borderline clients will, at times, cause tremendous problems in groups, these problems can be handled with skill and persistence. Clients with major "central processing" problems (severe brain damage and psychoses) plus an addiction are not suitable members for the kind of therapeutic group described in this book until their central processing problems are resolved or ameliorated.

The members of the group will determine the group's character; it would of course be ideal if one could pick and choose the members carefully so as to obtain the optimum group. One therapist might choose only very high socio-economic, stable clients who are highly motivated. Another therapist might prefer an issue-producing, healthy mix of men and women, old and young. However, most therapists working with addiction problems do not have that much freedom to create an "ideal" group. Our clients come to us in dire need and there is little possibility to pick and choose.

A group's composition and maintenance vary according to the kind of treatment program or facility. In an in-patient program, the group may be an "open group" (some members may be leaving and others coming into the group at the same time). Here, the group maintains about the same size, but there is continual change in individual membership and, of course, character.

Group management requirements will be very different if the group composition is continually changing as opposed to staying relatively stable. The principle to follow is that the more often the character of the group changes, the more active the therapist will have to become in order to achieve significant progress. In the short run this refers to both the orientation and the working periods of group therapy. For example, with an outpatient group which meets daily, and whose entire composition sometimes changes within two to three days, it is unreasonable to expect that the therapist will be able to gradually withdraw leadership and let the group assume leadership of itself. On the contrary, we would expect that the therapist would exert a much more definite and continuing role that would be short-term and goal-directed. If a client is going to be in a group for only two or three days, then the therapist must structure the group and exert strong management in order for the group to accomplish anything of significance.

This book is intended more for inpatient/outpatient groups which have some cohesion and stability built into them. These are the groups whose memberships are fairly stable at least over a period of weeks, months or even years.

GETTING STARTED[1]

Let's assume that we have a fairly stable and consistent population to work with. Our first task is to help group members get to know each other and begin to feel comfortable together. Addicted persons often enter a

---

[1]As an aid to preparing addicts for group psychotherapy I have authored a video entitled, *A Client Orientation to Group Therapy* (Bradenton, FL: Human Services Institute, 1990). Through dramatizations, this video explains and illustrates effective ways of participating in therapeutic groups. Viewing and discussing this video helps establish a basic set of ground rules and provides a positive framework for client involvement.

group with low self-esteem, strong defenses, a great deal of shame, guilt, paranoia and high anxiety. They often feel they are the only people in the world who cannot control their addictions. They feel alone and alienated. Picture how you yourself would react if you thought you were about to be exposed to a group as a reprehensible creature who cannot control his drugs or "booze." You'd probably be very afraid, defensive, and openly hostile, feeling as if people were "out to get you" or were going to ridicule you. These attitudes would make you resistent to change and, if there were others like you, a very resistive and hostile group would result.

The first thing we want to do, therefore, is "break the ice," to help the group members get to know each others' names and a little information about each other. There are many ways to do this, and I encourage you to be creative. One easy way to break the ice is a game called the "name game." In this game, clients are seated in a circle. One starts by thinking of an animal with the first letter being the same as the first letter in his first name, for example, by saying "my name is Impala Ivan." The game proceeds to the next person in the circle; that person introduces "Impala Ivan" to the group and adds that he is "Leopard Leo." The third client in the circle introduces "Impala Ivan" and "Leopard Leo" to the group and introduces himself as "Walrus Willy," and the game continues around back to the first person. Each succeeding person has more and more people to introduce; this causes some anxiety and anxiety-releasing laughter, which helps to reduce group tensions. (Incidentally, this game is also a good indicator of how well everyone in the group is detoxifying because it requires short-term memory to complete. However, anxiety or depression, as well as other conditions, can also cause a decrement in performance.) Besides helping group members become acquainted with each other, the "name game" or some other icebreaker begins the process of group members dealing directly with others in the group and performing in front of the group.

Next, it is important to gradually increase the level of intimacy among group members using several appropriate strategies and exercises. It is also good if the exercises can provide practice in some of the aspects of the group work to come. One exercise which fits both of these criteria is called the "Intimacy Game." In this exercise, the group is broken up into pairs or threesomes. Participants are given structured questions that they may ask of each other, with the stipulations that the answers are voluntary and that the information will be held confidential. Such a structured set of questions would tap different degrees of privacy, ranging from things like, "What's your favorite TV show?" to, "What's the most terrible thing you've ever done?" Some of the questions should contain items referencing drugs and alcohol, because many of the clients' feelings will center around these experiences.

The pairs or threesomes should spend about forty-five minutes asking and answering these questions, becoming comfortable with each other through this exercise in personal intimacy. Then the pairs should reassemble as a group and, without discussing the content of their answers, begin to discuss what happened during this exercise and how they felt about it. If things go well, this "processing" of the exercise will reveal several stages of growth. Clients usually report that at first they didn't think they had anything in common with their partners and were quite anxious about answering any of the more intimate questions. However, as they began to talk, they discovered that they had much in common, particularly in regard to their addictions. Further, they found that as one of them shared emotions or thoughts, the other tended to open up and also share more of his emotions. By the end of this exercise, group members usually feel more comfortable, more trusting, and "closer."

The client insights I just described don't arise spontaneously, however. The therapist must guide the discussion, as the following example shows:

[Therapist]: [To partners Mr. S. and Charlie] How did you feel about this game where you answered each others' questions?

[Mr. S.]: At first, I didn't want to answer, because I had thought Charlie didn't like me. But Charlie shared some really intense experiences with me. So I found out that he and I have a lot in common. Once I found that out, I felt more like trusting him. Then we spent most of the time just talking, not about the questions though.

[Therapist]: Would you say that you feel different about Charlie now?

[Mr. S.]: Definitely.

[Therapist]: How?

[Mr. S.]: Well, for one thing, I now feel like I know Charlie . . . much closer to him, and I think he feels much the same. He's someone I could talk with about my problems.

Following the discussion of how each person felt before, during, and after the exercise, the therapist could explain how this exercise is like group therapy. The therapist might say something like, "We are all a little apprehensive about sharing ourselves with others, but as we open up and share our feelings, trusting others, we begin to see that they are much like us and that we have a lot in common. By sharing our emotions and inner selves, we become closer to others, that is, develop intimacy. This prepares us to share our problems and get their feedback."

This intimacy exercise could also be repeated for several group sessions, with the only difference being that members could pair up with new partners each time. It is always best for the partners to be paired with those in the group they know least.

This intimacy exercise, or something like it, leads to a discussion of the primary prerequisite for a Friendly Forces group: trust. Most of the problems that develop within Friendly Forces therapy and other forms of therapy stem from a distrust between one or more group members. Without trust, a client can't begin to open up and won't feel comfortable giving feedback to others. Clients who lack trust may show behaviors ranging from denial to blatant acting out and disruption. In my experience, problems of trust account for the majority of reasons why a group fails to grow and develop, or reaches a significant impasse. Therefore, it is important to address this issue early.

One way to introduce the idea of trust is to ask members if knowing that their conversations would be confidential helped them to open up to each other during the "Intimacy Game." In most cases, they say that the confidentiality rule helped. Our own experiences with friends confirms this, too. We certainly wouldn't tell our friends many of the things we confide in them if we thought they would go out and discuss these with everyone they know. This point brings us to one of the cardinal rules of a Friendly Forces group: *whatever happens in the group remains confidential to the therapist and the group*, with the exception that certain other program professionals will know about the group development from the therapist's notes. However, all professional staff members in any legitimate treatment facility would be required to maintain client information as confidential.

The rule of confidentiality must be thoroughly discussed with the group. All group members should have an opportunity to openly and firmly commit to the rule of maintaining trust in the confidentiality of the proceedings. This is not to say that group members shouldn't discuss group therapy among themselves after the session. We want them to think about what happened in group therapy as much as possible. It simply means that the proceedings of group therapy shouldn't be discussed with anyone other than the professional staff or group members.

Sometimes, discussions of the trust issue can be aided by various exercises. You can use the ones I will describe or you can use your own creativity and design your own exercises. One exercise I use is called the "Trust Fall." At least two professional staff are required to be present. The therapist begins by sending all the group members out of the room and closing the door. Then the therapist asks one group member to come in, closing the door so that the others outside cannot see what is happening. The therapist tells the group member to turn away from him and the other staff member at a distance of about one to two feet and then says, "Close your eyes and fall backwards." As the client falls backwards slightly, the staff "catch" the client to prevent him from falling to the floor. The next client is brought in and repeats this exercise, while the client who has just participated joins the staff in catching him. This exercise is repeated until the whole group has completed it.

In another exercise called the "Trust Walk" the therapist has clients pair up. One partner is blindfolded and the other partner leads the blindfolded one around the building or campus for 15-20 minutes, helping him avoid injury and mishap. Note that these exercises require good judgment by the therapist. A client could easily be injured if the therapist isn't careful. For example, we certainly don't want a 350-pound man to come in first and have two female staff members, both weighing 95 pounds, try to prevent him from falling to the floor. Similarly, we don't want to have a very incompletely-detoxified person (still having trouble balancing) to lead around a blindfolded person, because he might not be able to adequately protect the blindfolded client.

Another interesting facet of such exercises is that sometime they will highlight a person who is already having trouble with trust. I have seen extremely distrustful persons simply refuse to do the "Trust Fall" or "Trust Walk." This gives the therapist diagnostic information about that person's problems and how he may interact in the group. Of course, after the therapist has completed the exercises, the results should be discussed in the group:

[Therapist]: What did you think of that exercise?" [Trust Fall].

[Mr. D.]: I was nervous when you asked me to close my eyes and fall backwards——I knew somehow that you'd catch me or something, but I was still worried.

[Mrs. C.]: [Who refused to participate] I don't think you should ask us to do these things. It's stupid. I don't know what this has to do with me being a cocaine addict.

[Mr. S.]: I think you [Mrs. C.] just didn't trust us to catch you. I was a little scared too, though. I guess that's something

I'll have to work on in this group, if we're going to trust each other.

[Therapist]: Good point. If you are going to become a close group, you have to take some risks to see if you can trust each other. If you don't trust each other, you won't participate in the group, and that'll mean you're not going to open up and really talk about yourselves.

[Ms. T.]: There's something else. If I feel others aren't opening up, then, I think I'll close up myself—because if others don't trust me, then I doubt I'll be able to trust them.

[Therapist]: If you see distrust in the group, you may want to bring it up so we can discuss it and try to resolve it. It's very important to bring up trust issues and in fact, to bring up any issue which you see interfering with the free flow of honest feelings.

Trust is probably the most important factor in a group; anytime the group seems to be significantly derailing or not reaching its potential, you should consider whether there is a trust issue involved.

The next two or three sessions could be a more formal outline of how the group therapy process will work. In some cases, this could be done by showing a videotape explaining the Friendly Forces model and procedures in detail, or the explanation could be given by the therapist in the group. The main point is to convey the information as clearly as possible.

First, the explanation of group psychotherapy should tell a little about psychological factors and addiction. The main point here is to convey the concept that addictions are "choice" behaviors motivated (but not absolutely determined) by psychological, social, and genetic factors. Group therapy should not be seen by the clients as a way to find the "cause" of their drinking, but as a way to examine and change the psychosocial factors, making it easier to choose not to drink or drug. If this distinction is not made clear in the beginning, groups will become stuck discussing drinking/drugging behavior, searching for a single event which caused the addiction.

Next, talk about "why group therapy," instead of individual therapy or some other modality. Emphasize denial and the other strong defenses of the addict. Whenever possible, draw upon the clients' own experiences, such as the difficulty they may have had admitting they needed treatment, and the losses they had to incur. This makes it easy to see that strong defenses often require strong group confrontation.

After this overview of the reasons for group psychotherapy, the therapist should explain the basic features of presentation, feedback, and the hoped-for dialogue between the presenter and the rest of the group. A presentation should last from thirty to forty-five minutes. This allows approximately the same amount of time for feedback from the group. A presentation should take the form of a life story, starting with early memories and moving through the years up to the present. It should cover important life stages and events: early childhood, adolescence, early adulthood, marriage (divorce), births of children, middle-age issues, and retirement. It should go beyond a simple reciting of facts and events, though, and describe how these events and stages affected one emotionally. I recommend that the addictive behavior be mentioned and tracked in its progression, but by all means you do not want a "drunkalogue" or a "drugalogue." Drunkalogues and drugalogues are presentations wherein the presenter focuses only on his addiction, talking about his drinking or drugging and nothing else. Such presentations tell us very little about the presenter as a person. We want the presenter to tell us about himself as a person: what motivates him, his emotions, and what has happened to him psychosocially.

The presenter should make a spontaneous presentation. Although he might think about what he is going to say, it is best not to plan ahead in too much detail. Planning a presentation too carefully hampers the spontaneous flow of emotions. These spontaneous emotions can be more revealing than any factual material a client might present. Explain that a presentation, if honest, may make one feel uncomfortable, because revealing the inner self that has been kept secret arouses anxiety, just as in the intimacy exercises discussed earlier. In fact, clients should realize that if they feel too comfortable during a presentation, they are probably not working very hard nor accomplishing very much. Group psychotherapy is like surgery. Surgery may be painful, or at least leave you feeling sore and uncomfortable, but you ultimately feel better and are healthier for having had the operation.

5

The Powerful Group
SHAPING AND DIRECTING IT

A basic rule for creating an effective and powerful therapy group for addicts is that each client should have at least one entire group session focused upon him and him alone. This forces each client to confront his own denial and avoidance. Because of their denial, many addicted persons will prefer an "open" type of group, which discusses general recovery topics such as "honesty"; within this format, members participate as they desire. This type of group is preferred by addicts because they can quickly "fade into the woodwork," avoiding any personalization of the material by refusing to relate it directly to their own lives.

In a general group discussion, a member could avoid participating and instead spend the hour daydreaming about going to the beach on the weekend. Or, the group might have a very long philosophical discussion of how it is best to be honest, but never confront members who are blatantly dishonest and suffer negative effects from it. But if one whole group session is focused on one person who presents information, then it will be very hard for him to avoid coming to grips with his problems. When he talks about himself the group will give him feedback about his unique situation.

No matter what the presenter does, it will probably result in some useful feedback from the group. For example, if the presenter skillfully avoids mentioning any emotions, the group will probably notice and mention it. This may lead to a self-awareness of the degree to which avoidance is itself a very significant problem in the presenter's life. In fact, much of the early group work is "resistance work." During this early stage, the major feedback the members may receive is that they are resisting the process. They may not be opening up and dealing directly with their emotions, which is one of the addict's foremost problems.

During his allotted session, the selected person will spend thirty to forty-five minutes presenting his life story, giving a chronological history of his major life events and their emotional impact upon him. We hope that during this presentation, the person will honestly reveal his problems, feelings, conflicts, and other aspects of his personality so that the group will be able to offer feedback about problem behaviors, for instance, recurring episodes of explosive behavior following a long period of repressed/suppressed anger, or continual moving and relocation that is clearly "running away from self."

The presentation and group feedback is a direct antidote to several problems. It encourages addicts to think about their emotional lives, something they are not generally prone to do. It encourages them to take responsibility for assessing and clarifying their problems, when the usual strategy is often to blame others and depend on them excessively. And it encourages them to become actively involved with others.

Following the presentation, and for about the same length of time, the group gives feedback. This is nothing other than their honest opinions about what they see occurring emotionally and behaviorally in the person who has just presented his life story. This processing of the presentation and the analysis of what is "going wrong" encourages the group members to address the presenter and his problems directly, relating to him in a therapeutic, straightforward manner and providing him with useful information about the way he communicates, how he deals with others, and his opinion about himself.

It is hoped that this uncomplicated process will lead to an open exchange between the presenter and the group wherein both continue to explore and deepen their understanding of how emotional conflict and behavioral problems develop. In a truly therapeutic group, this focus will continue throughout the remainder of the client's stay in the program.

THE THERAPIST'S ROLE

In a powerful therapeutic group, the therapist functions as a group manager or facilitator, with the ultimate intention of completely "fading out" of the process so that the group assumes full responsibility for its progress. The therapist is not there to lead the group discussion. If the group really solidifies into an independently functioning, organized whole, then the therapist can fade out of the process so as to further increase the group's power. Of course, during the group's formative period, the therapist will interact with the group or make "interventions." An intervention is a procedure wherein a therapist interrupts the normal flow of the group in order to redirect the group toward something it is overlooking. Such interventions arise from a group's inability to correct itself and stay on a course which will assure powerful communication from the group to the presenter.

The goal of every intervention is to return maximum responsibility to the group. Many addicts have spent a good deal of time avoiding responsibility, particularly for their feelings, and blaming others. Naturally, the first inclination of the group will be to look to the group "leader" (the professional) for guidance and direction, if not direct advice. We must realize that often the addict desperately wants the therapist to "take over" and interpret, guide, and advise. This removes the pressure from the client and prevents him from having to grow. To refer to our earlier analysis of a person tuning out his inner life: any time the therapist imposes structure or gives advice and guidance, the client is prevented from having to examine his inner life. The client no longer has to test his feelings and his will to act. He can simply follow the advice given to him and avoid any inner struggle or coming to terms with internal conflict. Think carefully and you will realize that most advice is designed to dictate some external action—reducing internal conflict and pushing things more to the outside. Let's look at an example of a poor intervention:

[Mr. K.]: [Winds up presentation] That's about all I can tell you. [Long silence of about 90 seconds with no one in the group saying anything].

[Therapist]: I'll start the feedback—I think you're depressed and that your depression comes from the fact that you get angry about a lot of things and you sit on it, reacting passively to the anger.

[Mr. B.]: Yeah, I agree with the counselor—I think you're too dependent. [Other group members chime in and repeat this feedback].

Notice what happened. By setting a precedent for being the first one to give feedback, the therapist removed a significant confidence-building occasion: the time immediately following the end of the presentation when group members themselves could learn to begin the feedback. Those who are passive and don't want to reveal their own feelings can now mimic the therapist's feedback and claim it as their own. Further, an authoritarian structure has been created wherein the group looks to the therapist to "lead off" the feedback.

Taking charge may benefit the therapist more than the group. The therapist may be relieving his anxiety about the silence and his doubts about the abilities of the group to handle the situation. By "rescuing" the group and taking responsibility to keep it moving, the therapist protects himself from his own feelings and insecurities. However, the therapist has also confirmed his doubts about the group's capabilities. Unfortunately, the group will sense those doubts at some level, creating other anxiety-arousing situations on later occasions during treatment. Now look at how this could have been handled better.

[Mr. K.]: [Winds up presentation] That's about all I can tell you. [Long silence with no one in the group saying anything].

[Therapist]: [Waits until 3 minutes have passed and then says to the Presenter] Maybe you had better find out from the group why you're not getting any feedback.

Notice the difference between this intervention and the previous example. This intervention places the responsibility on the presenter for finding out why he isn't getting feedback and on the group for dealing with the answer to that question. The intervention also gets the group to focus on resistance, instead of skipping over the resistance as the first intervention did. This practice follows the sound psychotherapeutic principle of analyzing and dealing with resistance before dealing with content. In other words, if a client is resisting saying something in the group, then it is better to first explore the resistance and later to deal with what the client was going to say (content). Analyzing and dealing with the resistance tells us important things about the client; we don't want to miss these or leapfrog over them. For example:

[Tony]: I just don't want to present today. Let me wait until tomorrow and I'll be happy to present then.

[Therapist]: What's going on that you don't want to present?

[Tony]: Well, I just don't want to present. I don't feel up to it.

[Therapist]: Why don't you get some feedback from the group on this point.

[Mickey]: I think you're avoiding, just like you do in the rest of the program. You always sit at the back of a room if you can and usually in here you try to sit outside the circle, but the counselor always asks you to come on down and join the rest of us. I overheard you telling Kevin that you were going to try to get out of presenting today and I think that's half of your problem in life—you avoid and don't face what you know that you should.

[Kevin]: I agree of course. I don't like to 'rat' on you Tony, but what Mickey said is true. You did tell me you were going to try to get out of the presentation and let Mickey take the responsibility for today.

Here, the presenter learns as much or more from the group analyzing his resistance than he probably would from the presentation itself. One of his most difficult problems is his avoidance of conflict. This suggests that he needs to go ahead and present in order to begin a new strategy: confronting problems and unpleasant situations. This intervention also establishes a precedent for the presenter and the group to take responsibility for this situation the next time it occurs.

Every intervention should be conducted so as to lessen the need for further interventions of that type. This principle follows from the principle immediately above. Interventions that are repeated are indications that the therapist has assumed a role of responsibility for the group, thus lessening the potential growth for the group. Often, the therapist spends a lot of time encouraging group members to become more involved with the presentation. Sometimes this is acceptable. But if it continues, using the same interventions over and over, then the therapist is maintaining a function which the group could undertake itself.

These first two principles can be quickly summarized by saying that when the therapist is doing a lot of talking, it's pretty clear that the group is not assuming enough responsibility and probably is not growing very much. The therapist's intervention can become a substitute for the clients risking an expression of their own inner feelings.

Here is another example:

[The presentation is very "dry" without much feeling and goes on and on describing fairly meaningless details. The presenter is really not telling much about himself].

[Therapist]:   [Interrupting the presentation]. Alice, maybe you should find out from the group whether you are telling them anything they can give you meaningful feedback on later.

This intervention is acceptable if, after it is done a few times, the group then begins to pick up the idea and performs the intervention itself. If the therapist intervenes every time a meaningless presentation occurs, the group will slowly come to depend upon the therapist to accomplish this function; the clients will not respond or deal with their feelings of anger, boredom, resentment, or nervousness. If this happens, the therapist may say something like:

[Therapist]:   Why do I have to keep interrupting the presentation when it is fairly clear to everyone that there isn't going to be anything to give feedback on later?

Then, the group and therapist would process the feelings and resistance of the group to becoming more assertive and confronting with the presenters, as demonstrated by the following.

[Mr. M.]:   I didn't know that we could interrupt the presenter. And I really don't like to do that kind of thing anyway—seems like a person ought to be able to present however he wants.

[Mr. W.]: You know, I get angry when I have to listen to all this garbage which I know doesn't mean anything. I get bored and sleepy——I felt like leaving the room and just not coming back.

[Therapist]: [To Mr. W.] So why not say something about it——say you're angry, bored, and sleepy because you know the feedback isn't going to be productive.

[Mr. W.]: Well, you hate to hurt the guy's feelings. And then I keep thinking maybe he'll say something important, but I guess that's wishful thinking. I also thought you guys [therapists] would stop the presentation and help the presenter express himself better.

[Therapist]: The more you become involved with structuring the group and the more you say what you think, the more you will benefit. If we simply take care of everything for you, you won't learn to stand up for your feelings. You'll become dependent on us. You'll just learn to continue to sit on your feelings.

[Mr. W.]: I think we should say something when the presenter isn't really bringing out what is bothering him because that's going to help us bring out what is really bugging us, too.

[Mr. M.]: I agree with you——it's really a waste to sit here and let someone bore us when we know that it's not going to help him. We need say, "you're not working the model."

[Therapist]: Okay, it seems that you have realized the point——if you have feelings about something going on in group, then you have a right to bring up those feelings and discuss them. In fact, this will help you grow and learn to take care of yourself emotionally. We're not

going to take care of this problem for you, so you
should begin to develop those skills now.

The therapist has tried to make additional interventions unnecessary by encouraging the group members to
assume greater responsibility. It is hoped that this will lead
to their taking on that responsibility and assertively
expressing themselves.

Therapist interventions should be guided by the
progress of the group. If the group is growing and developing at a reliable rate, the therapist should "keep hands off"
and fade out. If the group starts to stall and seems truly
stuck, or if something is happening that is clearly beyond
the sophistication of the group and likely to remain so,
then the therapist should intervene. Again, the group
cannot learn to take increasing amounts of responsibility
if the therapist doesn't provide opportunities for this to
occur. The following is an example of how this might be
done:

[Mr. C.]:   [To Therapist] Don't you think something in group has
gone wrong? I mean everyone is asking questions and
we don't seem to be getting anywhere.

[Therapist]:   [Assessing that the group may be able to process
this] What do you think about what's happening—why
don't you talk about it.

[Mr. C.]:   What do you guys think—are we on the track or not?

[Ms. B.]:   I don't think so—we've been asking questions for twenty
minutes or so and we still don't know anything about
how Jim felt about his childhood, his marriage or
anything else. I think he ought to present again later

after talking with some people about how to give a good presentation.

[Ms. W.]: Yeah, I was just thinking about the Group Psychotherapy Orientation film we saw last week. I remember it said that asking questions doesn't tell you about the presenter. I think that's what's happened here today—we fell into the trap of asking questions.

[Therapist]: That about sums it up. Why don't we take a break and leave it at that for the day. Jim can get with some of the more advanced group members and work on getting ready for a new presentation next week.

Here, the therapist assessed the group, let them try to process this incident alone, and the best positive outcome occurred. They realized what had happened to them and why they were frustrated. Then they gave this feedback to the presenter in such a way that it will be difficult for him to believe that he has really confronted his problems.

The power of the group is in the group—anything which drains off that power, cohesion, activity, or energy weakens it. Anything enhancing its activity and energy strengthens it. The professional therapist's role is to further the release of energy from the group members, but it should be a controlled release that is assertive and increases the bonds among the group members. Look at the following illustration:

[Mr. N.]: I'm done and ready for feedback about myself.

[Phillip]: You're just too nice to everyone for your own good—you never tell anyone what you really think.

[Jane]: [To Phillip] I disagree——I think that he speaks out, but no one will listen to him and the fault is mainly in his family, like his cold wife.

[Phillip and Jane begin a long discussion with each other and the feedback stops]

[Therapist]: What's going on in group today? What's happening to the feedback right now?

[Mr. A.]: Feedback's stopped. I think Jane and Phillip are debating. They should be talking with the presenter, not about him.

[Mr. C.]: You're right. And I think Jane is rescuing the presenter from the feedback . . . making excuses for him and shifting the feedback from him by her disagreement with Phillip. I think we should get back on track.

Notice here that the therapist could have simply told the group that they needed to talk directly with the presenter and by-passed any discussion of the dynamics taking place in the group. Instead, the therapist encouraged the group to examine itself, so as to learn about itself and the way its members are approaching problem solving. This self-examination, by the group members, strengthens the group and makes it more cohesive. Such an approach requires a therapist who feels good about himself and trusts the group. If he needs to bolster his ego by assuming authority and telling group members what to do, or if he doubts the ability of the group to handle the situation, then he will become much more active and prevent the group from attaining its potential strength. Repeated therapist interventions that are merely expressions of the therapist's inner concerns can block the growth of the client's inner consciousness just as the overprotective parent can hinder the growth of the child.

Only the members of the group can decide that they are a group. Only the group members can decide to struggle with their conflicts collectively and resolve those conflicts so that they become a more united force. It is not our role as therapists to *lead* the group per se, but instead to *facilitate* members dealing with each other in an increasingly honest and open manner. Ultimately, group members should feel that anything can be openly discussed in the group.

Every group has its limitations. For example, some groups will be ready to work and will achieve a great deal of growth. Some groups will not be ready to work and, in some cases, no matter what the therapist does, nothing much will change. This does not mean that the therapist is not an effective change agent, but is a realistic appraisal of his position in certain types of groups. To repeat myself, the power of the group is in the group. When we exceed an objective assessment of our own power as therapists, then we begin to feel that we can make the group function. A realization that we have failed to do so with a particular group can lead to reactions of anger and depression.

Although our job is to help concentrate the group's power and refine it, we cannot overcome ardent resistance, at least not in a short inpatient facility or time-limited outpatient group, and perhaps, not at all. As a review of the literature will show, many addicted persons will not improve with treatment. This is something we don't understand, but it is a fact. This is not to say that we should ever give up on any individual or group when there is still any hope whatsoever of achieving progress. Rather, we need to be aware of our limitations and not set our expectations too high. If we do, we may react to clients and groups very negatively and hence, may actually end up being antitherapeutic. Later on in this book, I will describe what I feel our criteria for "feeling good" about our group work should be. In brief, I think that we must reward ourselves for doing what is best for the client and the group and focus primarily on this, rather than on the immediate success of our efforts.

6

Feedback
THE KEY TO SUCCESSFUL GROUP THERAPY

Feedback is a group member's honest reaction to the presenter. It is based both on the content of the presentation and the previous experiences group members have had with the presenter.

The therapist should stress that the presenter must open up to benefit from feedback. The more open and honest the presentation, the better the feedback will be. Underscore that the group member should put his feedback in his own words; many clients will assume that they have to come up with a very sophisticated psychological interpretation of behavior or appear to be very educated. All group members should be aware that they will certainly have some kind of opinion about the presenter after living with him for several days (in the case of an inpatient facility) or after hearing his presentation. Here are some examples of good feedback:

[Mr. R.]: That's about all I can tell you about my life. I'm ready for feedback.

[Mr. N.]: It's pretty apparent that your early life experiences left you feeling very inadequate. I think this came somewhat from your dad, since he was always unhappy with you and never showed you any love at all. So, I wasn't surprised when you chose to stay in your little home town rather than accept that four-year football scholarship——you were afraid to leave home and so you learned to avoid things for fear of failure. Now, you hate yourself for not having tried to get your education and accomplish more than you have, so you continue to be critical of yourself, lowering your self-confidence further. You even call yourself the black sheep of your family. You showed that same avoidance today, because you tried to get out of presenting in group, tried to get Mr. G. to present. No wonder drinking is so attractive to you when you feel like such a failure. I'll pass, and let someone else tell you their opinion.

[Ms. L.]: I agree with that and I see more of the same patterns. You and Joe had a run-in the other day, when you thought he was making slurs about your race. All us group members told you to talk with him about it and I even heard some of the staff encouraging you, too. But you've avoided the problem and simply stayed away from Joe . . . talking about him behind his back. I also saw you wouldn't give him feedback the other day when he presented, so I think you're definitely still angry.

When group members provide feedback they should maintain good eye contact, looking directly at the presenter. In the following example, the therapist reminds a group member to do this:

[Marie]: [Giving feedback, but looking out the window] And I think you are still angry with your ex-wife and still want to get revenge on her . . .

[Therapist]: Who are you talking to, Marie?

[Marie]: Why Bob, of course.

[Therapist]: Then why don't you look at him while you're speaking to him, so that he'll be sure you are talking to him and not someone else.

Maintaining eye contact develops a stronger feeling of intimacy and personalizes the message, resulting in a more powerful communication. For the same reasons, we encourage group members to make "I" and "you" statements, speaking directly to the presenter. Here is an example of how a therapist deals with the need to personalize statements:

[Ted]: I'm through with my presentation and ready for your feedback.

[Ms. Y.]: He's still torn up over the death of his wife and can't grieve because he thinks it is not manly to cry and be depressed—so instead he's drinking and drugging away his depression . . . avoiding the reality that his wife is gone.

[Therapist]: [To Ms. Y.] Why don't you repeat that feedback to Ted [the presenter] and talk directly to him, saying 'I think you,' using 'I' and 'you' statements so that you are talking to him, not about him.

We want the group members giving feedback to relate directly to the presenter instead of talking to the group about the presenter. This helps establish a pattern of dealing directly with people. Some therapists may feel such interventions are somewhat "picky" and feel uncomfortable making them. However, we must remember that the power of feedback is cumulative. Intervening to increase the directness of a client's feedback results in a more productive group and better personal growth.

Group members should realize that feedback is a statement, not a question. While not absolutely prohibited, questions are strongly discouraged. Let's look at the following interaction:

[Mr. S.]:   I know I've only talked for 12 minutes, but really not much of importance has happened in my life and I just can't think of anything else to say. I'm ready for feedback.

[Ms. G.]:   I didn't really understand what happened in your childhood—where was your mother and why did your grandmother raise you?

[Mr. S.]:   I really don't know what happened to my mother—my grandmother wouldn't ever talk about her much and dad always said she was 'just a bitch.'

[Mr. D.]:   What ever happened to your two kids—you mentioned a divorce, but never mentioned your kids again—what happened?

[Mr. S.]:   My ex-wife got remarried and moved to Texas, and I haven't heard from the kids in over 15 years. After a while I just figured they were better off without me.

Notice what happened. The whole group process has been turned upside down. Instead of the presenter taking responsibility for his life and feelings, he basically avoided the whole problem by shifting the responsibility to the group for finding the factors contributing to his addiction.

Moreover, the group accepted the responsibility for obtaining information from him instead of confronting his failure to reveal his emotions and experiences. If the presenter actually sets the group up to ask questions, it is very unlikely that these questions will result in any useful information. The presenter probably has have already decided not to be open about himself. No matter how many questions the group asks they may still not ask the "right" ones, those which will bring forth the events and feelings that the presenter really needs to deal with.

Now that the presenter has grabbed control of the process by setting up the group to ask questions after his sketchy presentation, he can sit back and relax, spending the remainder of the session telling only enough about himself to tease them and keep them asking questions. Since the group will not obtain enough valid information to provide feedback, the presenter will not have to face any uncomfortable feedback or deal with real issues in his life. It is not up to the group to "pull out" the problems from the presenter. The following example shows an effective group response to this problem:

[Mr. S.]: [Ending presentation] I know I've only talked for 12 minutes, but really not much of importance has happened in my life and I just can't think of anything else to say.

[Ms. G.]: To be honest, you really haven't told us anything. I suggest you start over and tell about the important things in your life, how you felt about them. Or, maybe you should wait a couple of days and get some help from other people in the group.

[Mr. D.]: I agree. You're just not dealing with your life. If you don't get involved in your own life, how can we help you with it?

Encourage "assertive" feedback but emphasize that feedback is not a vehicle for expressing personal feelings of anger or for taking revenge on someone in the group. Take the following example:

[Mr. S.]:   [Concluding presentation] Well, that's about it.

[Mr. L.]:   You've been no good since the day you were born, haven't you? You were a juvenile delinquent, a rebel in the service, and have done all kinds of illegal things since then ... including 'dealing drugs.' I can definitely understand why your wife divorced you. How do you think you can ever be accepted by others if you're always doing illegal and antisocial things? You're just no damn good.

Mr. L. made some good feedback points, but his feedback was too hostile and will be reacted to emotionally. When feedback is hostile, the presenter becomes angry, distorting and misinterpreting the message. Aggressive feedback makes it easier for a defensive presenter to "write off" a message as weird or trivial. If the presenter accepts the moral criticism inherent in aggressive feedback—"you're just no good"—it may damage his self-concept and self-esteem, which are already very, very low. Encourage clients to make their feedback as assertive as possible but free from strident and unnecessary emotions. Here is an example of assertive feedback which is not overly aggressive:

[Ms. S.]: [Concluding presentation] So now it's your turn; I'm ready.

[Mr. M.]: I think your aggression has really caused you a problem. It seems like you've fought against authority . . . lots of times. You've either made very bad relationships for yourself or written off all the important ones you've had. Just like you said, you have been divorced four times and have just about given up on marriage. Maybe you should be more assertive and less aggressive.

Here, Mr. M. conveyed information in a very straightforward and factual manner. Now the presenter can focus on the content of the information, the facts, instead of the personal emotions it might arouse.

Emphasize that you expect each person to provide feedback during every session. When you emphasize the need to contribute feedback regularly and frequently, some group members will contend they "learn by listening" or that their A.A. or N.A. sponsor said, "God gave you two ears and one mouth so you could listen twice as much as you talk." In the Friendly Forces model of therapy, however, you can only "learn by doing"; this requires that group members all provide feedback so that they can begin to feel comfortable about being assertive.

Someone will invariably say, "I didn't give feedback because 'Joe' already said what I wanted to say and there's no use repeating feedback." You should disagree and say that repetition of feedback is important because it lets the presenter know what different group members are thinking. Without this feedback, even if it is repetitive, the presenter might conclude that a group member is uninterested in his presentation. The repetition of feedback gives it more force. If one person tells you you're too dependent, it's not too hard to shrug off. But if ten people all say that you're too dependent, that is powerful feedback and it can't be easily ignored or denied.

Feedback should avoid moral implications. Feedback isn't part of a referendum to decide whether a person is good or bad. Instead, try to point out objective information that will make certain contingencies clear for the presenter. Consider the following example:

[Mr. P.]:   So, when I was really drinking heavily, I found that I was beginning to get into deep trouble with my family. My wife and I would get into horrible fights and I would verbally, and later, physically abuse her. I never really hurt her bad, just slapped her around a little to scare her. I also started running around on her before I moved out. Later, I moved out and moved in with my mother. I really needed to anyway . . . my mother really depends on me.

[Ms. W.]:   You know, you're really a dog for living with your mother . . . and no self-respecting man would abuse his wife like that. And running around on your wife is adultery and sinful— why that's against the Scriptures and all morals—it's just not right to do that sort of thing. All I can see is that you're just no good.

This example illustrates a serious liability of moralistic feedback. What is actually happening is that one person's morals (Ms. W.'s) are being used to judge another person's behavior (Mr. P.s') *without mentioning the actual consequences of the behavior for the presenter*. From judging, it is easy to move to condemning, which we see in the above example: repeated attacks on Mr. P.'s worth, which will simply weaken his self-esteem further. Good feedback, in contrast, provides the presenter with information about what's going on inside of him and how this is motivating his behavior, which in turn affects how he feels about himself and others. Moralistic feedback, where someone uses his own moralistic standards to judge the behavior of another, does not provide this objective view of the presenter. Further, it tends to cause personal emotional reactions which interfere with objective processing of the feedback. A better sort of feedback, which provides more information, may be illustrated by the following:

[Mr. P.]: So, when I was really drinking heavily, I found that I was beginning to get into deep trouble with my family. My wife and I would get into horrible fights and I would verbally, and later, physically abuse her. I never really hurt her bad, just slapped her around a little to scare her. I also started running around on her before I moved out. Later, I moved out and moved in with my mother. I really needed to anyway . . . my mother really depends on me.

[Ms. W.]: I think that as your drinking progressed, you became more aggressive, trying to force others to act the way you wanted. If they didn't, you retaliated. Your aggression caused your marriage to deteriorate. Then there's your dependence. You had to move in with your mother. It seems like you needed your mother, and not the other way around. I feel that being too demanding and too dependent really caused a lot of your problems. I think it would help to work on these. If you continue to behave this way, you'll probably keep on having the same problems.

Notice that this nonmoralistic feedback doesn't even mention whether the presenter's behavior is "right" or "wrong," "righteous" or "sinful," "moral" or "immoral," "good" or "bad." These frames of reference are irrelevant to our job of creating a valuable group therapy experience for clients. Nonmoralistic feedback *assumes the presenter's innate self-worth and dignity* and proceeds to state some inner processes (demandingness, dependency) that appear to be tied to the problem behaviors (drinking, aggression, inordinately dependent living arrangements). Notice that the group member giving the feedback remains neutral about any necessity or urgency to change the behavior. She points out that the presenter can continue these patterns but will probably experience the same negative results. This nonmoralistic feedback leaves the presenter with the message that inner processes are connected with behaviors that, while neither right nor wrong, have very definite effects upon him. It is hoped that this message will leave the presenter motivated by a concern for himself and the interconnections of his feelings and behavior.

A final important point is that moralizing by group members tends to create layers of "moral inferiority/ superiority," within a group which alienate the members from each other and may even cause open hostility and aggression. When a group member spends all his time morally condemning others, those members feel "put down," and the moralizer feels superior and different from the others. Hence, he doesn't need to attend to what they have to say about him. Therapists who are prone to be moralizing run the risk of judging the clients and reacting to them negatively. This will certainly be felt by the clients, regardless of whether such views are ever verbalized.

You should insist that feedback be a statement of "what is happening" rather than "advice." Many, if not most, addicted persons have received tons of advice and have failed to follow it because they simply do not learn this way, or they habitually resist pressure from others. So, from a practical standpoint, advice isn't effective. More-over, when we give advice we tend to assume responsibility for solving someone's problem, rather than encouraging them to think for themselves and struggle to solve a problem. Worst of all, when we give advice we assume responsibility for any failure, something the addicted person often wants us to do: "Well, I did what you told me to do and I still wound up using drugs/alcohol."

Advice usually intends to solve a specific problem, such as getting a new job or moving. It is better that the group give the presenter more global information about his central functioning ("You're still so resentful about those past events"). The best feedback tells the presenter *how we see him functioning now*. The following examples will clarify this:

[Ms. C.]: So, when my mother-in-law moved in with us, I thought it would be a good arrangement, but she does things all the time that I just hate and yet, I can't say anything about it because my husband will get very upset.

[Mr. W.]: You should find a nursing home and then your husband will be happy that his mother is in the home . . . where she'll get excellent care.

[Mr. F.]: Or, you could stay in the room away from your mother-in-law when she's there. Just go work on a project or something, maybe a hobby. Then you wouldn't have any interaction with her.

Notice that the group members are suggesting a solution to the presenter's problem and therefore go directly to talking about the solution, rather than fully examining *what the presenter is doing to contribute to the problem*. The presenter is learning about general external problem-solving strategies, not about her emotions and behavior. General external problem-solving strategies are important, but they are not the most valuable outcome from group psychotherapy.

By offering to solve one particular problem for the presenter, the group members are discouraging an understanding of herself that might help her cope with other problems she has or will encounter. They are taking responsibility for choosing which behaviors the presenter should employ in solving her problems instead of trusting that she can make such choices herself. The following illustrates better feedback:

[Mrs. C.]: So, when my mother-in-law moved in with us, I thought it would be a good arrangement, but she does things all the time that I just hate and yet, I can't say anything about it because my husband will get very upset.

[Mr. W.]: I think this thing with you're mother-in-law is making you real unhappy. You're getting angry but not doing anything about it. Maybe you're too dependent on your husband and his opinions. Maybe this dependency's making you put up with problems you could solve and be rid of.

Notice how the responsibility has been very carefully placed back on the presenter—it is up to the client to find a solution to the problem and make choices accordingly. The feedback now provides a window into how her dependency and passivity obstruct a resolution of her problems.

There may be resistance by group members to avoiding advice-giving. One way to handle this is to ask the group, "How many of you have had a lot of advice?" This quickly reminds the group of how much unheeded advice they have gotten and how little good it has done them. One of the few contexts in which advice-giving is effective is where a clear relationship is noted between the advised action and a personal state of consciousness. For example, it would be helpful to advise, "You'd better move out of your mother's house *if you really want to assume more responsibility for yourself.*" Such advice links an action to the person's dynamics.

Highly effective feedback touches on emotions and feelings; it is not simply an intellectual statement of what is happening to the presenter.

[Mr. C.]:　You probably won't understand because most of you have not been in the upper circles of society like I was. And most of you probably haven't gone to college or to graduate school—but believe me, if you had stress like that, you'd drink too.

[Ms. B.]:　You know, John, I feel that one of your problems is that you treat others as if they were inferior. And then you think they ought to do exactly like you think they should. You're really disappointed when they don't live up to your expectations and you begin to distrust them. I know you make me feel inferior, so I want to avoid you. You always top any story I tell. That really hurts my feelings. Maybe you really feel inferior and have to look down on others to feel okay about yourself.

This group member has given feedback about the inner feelings of the presenter (feelings of superiority/inferiority) and how that leads to behavior (harsh criticism of others) that hurts others and redounds negatively in the end (others feel degraded and want to avoid/reject the presenter).

When the group members assertively express personal feelings as part of their feedback, it gives the presenter some potent intellectual and emotional/social information which causes him to pause and consider his assumptions about himself, others, and their impact upon his social relations. However, such personal feedback has to be given in a positive, helpful manner if it is to avoid raising the presenter's resistance. If the presenter receives the impression that the group members are using emotional statements to attack him, he will merely become angry, hurt, and defensive.

"Rescuing" is a statement or question designed to prevent the presenter from being hurt. Look at how rescuing works in the following example:

[Ms. D.]:   That's about it——I'm ready for feedback.

[Mr. F.]:   It seems you're much too dependent to ever develop your own talents——you've never really lived on your own in your entire life . . .

[Mr. S.]:   [Interrupting the feedback] But look, she [Mrs. D.] never had a chance to develop independence because her father was so critical she didn't have any self-confidence and her mother was always taking care of all the responsibilities——so how can you expect she'd have ever become independent.

[Mr. F.]:   Please let me continue. Besides being so dependent, you expect everyone to do as you want them to. But you don't make any efforts of your own . . .

[Mr. S.]:   [Interrupting again] But look, I don't see why her parents would have objected to her moving back in after her husband threw her out. They should have seen that her husband didn't give her much of a chance and should have tried harder to get her to stay sober.

Notice that the "rescuer" is actually not speaking to the presenter at all. He is "debating" or "deflecting" the feedback. Of course, the rescuer is trying to prevent the presenter from being "hurt" by the feedback or from being "criticized" by the feedback. Let's look at a more subtle form of rescuing in the following example:

[Mr. J.]: That's the way it is with me. I'm ready for feedback.

[Ms. T.]: I think you're much too dependent to ever develop your own talents. You've never lived on your own in your entire life . . .

[Mr. W.]: [Interrupting] But you know, I think we need to be talking about the drinking. I can see why you did the things you did. Alcohol was really getting a hold on you and you started doing a lot of destructive things. I know how you feel, I've done the same things myself. Yes sir, I think we need to focus on alcohol. That's why we're here.

Here, the rescuer is more subtle and just changes the subject (or may start asking very neutral and useless questions) to block further feedback. Another rescuing tactic is to interrupt the feedback for a moment and "derail" it. Rescuers have infinite means of rescuing the presenter, but the cardinal feature will be that *the rescuer tries to help the presenter avoid facing what appears to be a painful self-truth.* An astute therapist will quickly see those in the group who are prone to rescuing because this behavior is very obvious and consistent. Furthermore, it will quickly become apparent that those who rescue others don't want to face their own shortcomings and are hoping that others will rescue them, too. The rescuer's behavior is sometimes an offering to that bargain: "You don't confront me and I won't confront you."

Often a group member will rescue a presenter because he thinks this person is feeling bad. To nullify this tendency, a therapist should explain, "We are here to help you, not to make you feel good for the moment." The only way a group can help someone is to be assertively honest with its feedback. Encourage group members to ask the presenter about the effects of their feedback when they are concerned that it might make the presenter feel angry or offended. If a presenter seems to become angry about feedback, the group member(s) should certainly comment about his reaction and ask about the psychosocial factors at work.

THE THERAPIST'S ROLE IN FEEDBACK

The role of the therapist can be simply explained as "management" of the group in the event that the group doesn't manage itself. It should be made clear that the responsibility for the group's conduct and progress ultimately rests with the group itself, not the therapist. The assuming of responsibility must be strongly emphasized because most group members will tend to see the therapist as responsible, especially in the initial stages of the group process. They will want the therapist to actively lead them.

The group can be told that it is the therapist's function to intervene if the group process is not moving forward, so that the group can become more aware of that fact, and to occasionally provide feedback to the group and individual members about their progress. The following is an example of a therapist's early intervention:

[Ralph]: [Finishing presentation] Go ahead and give your feedback.

[Mr. J.]: Why did you quit that job you had in the United Kingdom? Was it because you felt you weren't being recognized for what you could do?

[Ralph]: No, I really didn't care about that. I was just tired of the job and wanted to do something else. So I decided to quit.

[Ms. M.]: And why have you moved around so much? Were you running away from something?

[Ralph]: No, I think I was just born with the wanderlust and start getting an itch now and then, just like most people. Don't you ever want to change or to do something different?

[Ms. S.]: What ever happened to your kids from your first marriage? You mentioned you left that family, but you never mentioned your children again.

[Therapist]: [Intervening] What's going on in group today? This is supposed to be a feedback period—are we giving feedback?—what's happened?

[Mr. D.]: We're asking questions because Ralph didn't give any information and we really don't have any feedback to give him.

[Therapist]: I think that is valid feedback. If you feel you don't have any information, why not give him that feedback.

At the close of the group session, the therapist might ask members why he had to stop the group and point out the questioning and lack of feedback. Why hadn't the group members picked up this trend and confronted themselves with it? What can they do if this happens again?

Therapist interventions are meant to make the group aware of its limitations and to provide direction for growth. Therapists should stress that it is hoped the group will learn to recognize when it is functioning at a level much below its capability. Repeat that group members should try to be spontaneous, speaking out if they have strong feelings about *any aspect of the group process*. If a group member is beginning to be bored by what is a very dry and emotionless presentation, then he should interrupt the presenter and tell him:

[Mr. C.]: I was raised by my mom and dad. My mom was a housewife and rather sickly. My dad was a workaholic . . . always on the road . . . I really never saw my dad very much. After high school, I entered the navy . . . in 1961. That year I trained on naval communications and did very well. In 1964, I was discharged from the navy and went to work for Jack's Brothers Distributors . . .

[Susan]: [Interrupting] Look, I'm finding this boring! You're just reciting facts and no details. I don't know anything about how you felt . . . as a child, how your family got along emotionally and where you fitted in, or anything else about what you liked and didn't like. I think you should start over and tell us what was been going on emotionally while these things were happening.

[Mr. Y.]: Yeah, I was thinking the same thing. I'm glad Susan had the guts to speak out and let you know that you're really not telling us anything that we're going to be able to give feedback on.

In this example, at least two group members had strong negative feelings about how the presentation was going but only one spoke up. Therapists should stress that if a group member has strong feelings about something in the group, then other people are probably having similar feelings, too. Here is another example:

[Arthur]: [Ending presentation] Go ahead with your feedback.

[Ms. P.]: I think you're a nice, likable guy and I don't see that you have any problems, except that you drink too much. If you could just stop drinking, it would sure go a long way toward curing you.

[Mr. S.]: I agree. We all like you very much and it's too bad about what your wife did. But maybe things will be better now.

[Ms. C.]: I don't have any feedback to give to you today. I just don't know what to say.

[Mr. W.]: I think the group is missing the point. Arthur has been cuddling up to you guys and even me, since the first time he got here. He buys you cigarettes, he's always wheeling Alex over to the laboratory. He even offered me some football tickets the other day . . . which I know his family wanted. I think this has really gotten to you guys and you don't want to give him feedback because he has bribed you, more or less. I just don't think it'll help him be dishonest.

So I'm going to give you feedback, Arthur [turning to the presenter]. You are a people-pleaser and you want others to like and take care of you. But you're such a doormat that others just lose respect for you and really don't want to be around you all that much . . . except to take advantage of you. You were hoping to use your favors so you wouldn't get feedback you don't want to hear, and it almost worked.

I think you really don't like yourself very much and you try to get others to like you to make up for it. I think it would help if you let the group members here know that you want them to be strictly honest, so you can really begin to work on your problems.

In both these situations there were mature group members who noticed some very difficult problems occurring in the presentations and group processes. Let's look at another example of a very mature group responding to a problem situation:

[Ricardo]:   [Finishing presentation] That's it. I'm ready for feedback.

[Ms. L.]:   I'm shocked about how you behaved with your family. It's appalling. Your wife was trying to help you and you wouldn't even stay faithful to her. So you have no one but yourself to blame. You weren't a good father to your kids and your job performance was way below what you could do.

[Mr. M.]:   [Interrupting] I think you ought to stop and consider what you [to Ms. L.] are doing. You told me that you really intended to "burn" Ricardo when it was his turn to present. And that is exactly what you're doing now. You're not giving constructive feedback, just trying to make Ricardo feel bad because you didn't like his feedback when you presented. So, I think you ought to stop and think about what you're saying.

In this situation, a more mature group member revealed a "hidden agenda" which could have had a destructive effect upon the quality of the therapy. Notice, incidentally, that this example shows clearly that only the group members can "form a group" and deal with the real problems of the group. If Mr. M had not volunteered this information, the therapist might never have known about it. In order for the group to assume increasing amounts of responsibility, the group members must be spontaneous in providing "process feedback." This helps the group make self-corrections.

At this point, in the group psychotherapy orientation, ask if there are any questions about the overall process. Usually, there will be just a few questions because most of the group members do not have enough experience to know what questions to ask. After these preliminary questions have been answered, pick someone to present during the next session to get the process started. Another option is to wait until the next group session to ask someone to present. Both methods have advantages and disadvantages, but I prefer to have someone predesignated as the next session's presenter. This gives the presenter time to get ready and the therapist time to review the details of that person's case records. The disadvantage of allowing someone to know that he will be presenting at the next session is that he may feel anxious about it. When this happens he may rehearse a very defensive presentation or overorganize his presentation.

There are a number of ways to decide who will present. You can ask for volunteers. You can ask the group to designate a presenter. Or, you can go by the sequence in which the clients were admitted to the program. I prefer to ask for a volunteer, keeping in mind that the volunteer ought to have been in the program long enough to be fairly well-oriented. Obviously, you don't want a volunteer who entered the program just the day before and doesn't even know the names of the other group members; it is quite unlikely that this person will feel comfortable, trust the group, or be able to open up easily.

This brings us to a point where we are ready for the first real presentation and to consider how therapists interact with the group.

7

Group Process
TECHNIQUES TO STRENGTHEN IT

Ideally, group therapy for addicts involves a multidisciplinary team. This is especially important if the therapist
is inexperienced. But even an experienced therapist,
working alone with a group, may miss a lot that is happening within a typical psychotherapy group of fourteen
clients.

It is advisable to have a multidisciplinary team con-
sisting of a counselor, a social worker, a psychologist, a
psychiatrist, and a nurse (or licensed practical nurse or
nursing assistant), to detect the multiple levels of interactions taking place in the group, something that would be
precluded by having staff members of only one discipline.
You can see how this works in the following example:

[Mr. G.]: My mother constantly criticized my father, particularly
because of his alcoholism. And she always would also
look at me and say 'You're just like your father and I
believe you'll turn out just like him.' It always made
me angry and upset and over the years, I became more

and more removed from women. Every time I got involved with a woman I would end up having very emotional arguments with her.

Here, a psychologist might focus more on what is going on from the personal, self-esteem point of view; his insights may be extremely useful to the client in individual therapy. A social worker might be more attentive to the family dynamics and how these may affect later social interactions; these observations will be valuable when the client's mother or current girlfriend comes in for family/conjoint therapy. A female nurse hearing the group presentation may have noticed that the client responded to her requests for medication checks with unusual anger. Now she has some hints as to why: perhaps it is precisely because she is a female authority figure that he has a conflict right away, before he even gets to know her.

DEFUSING CLIENT HOSTILITY

There is another major advantage of a team approach to group psychotherapy: it is easier to deal effectively with client resistance. Many groups of addicts are initially quite resistant and can become openly hostile toward the therapist. This often stems from their attempt to externalize—to avoid focusing on themselves. When this occurs, and if you are the only professional present, it becomes very difficult to avoid becoming defensive. A therapist working in isolation may not be able to remain calm enough to help group members work through their resistance; instead, he may actually encourage their externalization by reacting defensively. Here is an illustration of this phenomenon:

[Mr. C.]: [Talking to sole therapist] Look, you therapists just like to come in here and expose us. You never tell us anything about yourself. You don't say anything about your own feelings. It's just that clients have to tell all their dirty laundry, while you don't say a word about your mistakes. Why don't you present today and let us give you feedback?

[Therapist]: I'm being paid to deal with your problems, not my own. I admit I have my share and I could certainly benefit from working on them, but this is not the place.

[Ms. G.]: Yeah, you therapists feel like you are better than us and so you can come in here and hear a good story about someone and then laugh about it later.

[Therapist]: I assure you that's not true . . .

[Mr. U.]: Then let us know what your problems are if you believe in confidentiality.

[Therapist]: [Hesitating] I don't think that's any of your business right now. Now shut up and let's get on with the presentation!!!

The therapist was challenged by the group members and became defensive. As many of us do when on the defensive, he resorted to being authoritarian and impulsive. Notice how the group members effectively shifted the focus from themselves to the staff member. The therapist's defensiveness actually reinforced their feeling that therapists consider themselves "above" or superior to the group members. Now let's consider what happens when more than one therapist or professional staff is present:

[Mr. C.]:   [Talking to one of the staff members present] Well, look, you therapists just like to come in here and expose us. You never tell us anything about yourself. You don't say anything about your own feelings. It's just that clients have to tell all their dirty laundry, while you don't say a word about your mistakes. Why don't you present today and let us give you feedback?

[Therapist 1]:   I'm being paid to deal with your problems, not mine. I admit I have my share and I could certainly benefit from working on them, but this is not the place.

[Ms. G.]:   Yeah, you therapists feel like you are better than us and so you can come in here and hear a good story about someone and then laugh about it later.

[Therapist 2]:   Why are you focusing on the staff right now? You seem to feel that staff is doing something to you. What's going on?

[Mr. A.]:   We're uncomfortable, like we're fish in a bowl and you're looking in on us, making fun of us because we're exposed and you're not.

[Therapist 1]:   So, you're feeling pretty uncomfortable when you begin to talk about yourself?

[Mr. F.]:   Yes, and it feels pretty bad to think about what everyone on the staff must be thinking.

[Therapist 2]:   What do you think we're thinking?

[Mr. A.]:   You're thinking we're a bunch of hopeless people who'll never stop drinking and drugging.

[Therapist 1]:   No. We know you can change and we're not trying to be critical. But when people begin to open up in group, they often become fearful. Sometimes they're confronted by things they don't approve of in themselves. Then they expect criticism, especially from the staff. Believe me, we're in this to help you. We think you're good people who have just learned behaviors that aren't working for you. And we think you can learn a better, more constructive way.

[Therapist 2]:   Yes. Often when people first begin group and open up, they're frightened by their feelings. Their defensive reaction is to 'attack' anyone who might be around . . . to put the focus on someone else. I think that's what's happening to you today. You're feeling "exposed" and uncomfortable with some of your inner feelings. Instead of trying to put us on the spot, it might be better to work on accepting your own hurts and disappointments.

[Mr. A.]:   I guess you have something there, because I knew today was my day to present and I've really been feeling nervous about it. I stayed awake all night wondering whether to try to con the group or to try to be honest.

The preceding illustrates a very common dynamic. Often a group will become very apprehensive after a few presentations, during which the group gives good, confronting feedback. When this happens, several of the group members begin to realize the group is developing considerable force and that they, too, may have to face aspects of themselves they are quite unhappy and self-critical about. So, they may feel "cornered" and begin to lash out at the therapist. If this happens, it is very important for staff to remain nondefensive, skillfully helping the group members ask why they are reacting this way, how they are feeling, and what it is related to. These attacks can put a single therapist under considerable pressure. It is very important to have more than one therapist present to help shift the focus back onto the group members.

TEAM PLANNING

It is a very good idea for the professional team to meet ten or fifteen minutes before the group therapy session to discuss both the group's progress and the client who is presenting. In this meeting the team can consider what the group and the presenter are likely to do and how to handle it. For example, if the team feels that a dependent client is presenting, who will probably set the group up to ask continual questions, the staff might decide to intervene quickly and discourage questions. Or, they may want to let the group experience the frustrations of continual questions and learn to deal with it. Another possibility is that the staff may have noted continuing client resistance to giving feedback, or they may have noticed that the group members are overly sensitive to any suggestion that they are "rescuing." If these obvious "process" problems haven't been brought up for discussion, the team might decide to ask the group if they want to have an "open discussion" about how the group is going.

If a client is to present and the group seems ready, the team will probably want to use this preprocess group meeting to discuss what is known about him. The staff could review the psychiatrist's mental status exam, the counselor's interview with the client, the psychological test results, the social worker's family history assessment, and the nursing assessment. The object is for the team to be thoroughly familiar with the client's dynamics, problems, and the ways the group might react to him. This meeting also offers an opportunity to continue developing the staff liaisons and relationships that are so necessary for a therapeutic treatment team in an addictions treatment unit. The following are segments of a preprocess meeting which illustrate some of these principles:

[Counselor]: I talked with Al M___ [the presenter for that day] the other day and he told me he's a cocaine addict and that's his only problem. In fact, he said he's not sure he needs to stay longer in the program and maybe should just leave and attend Cocaine Anonymous. I got the impression that he is using a great deal of denial . . . that he's basically a very grandiose person who has a need to feel very powerful and doesn't see the connection between that need and his cocaine usage.

[Social Worker]: I talked with the wife and family. The parents are upper-middle-class and the father has been quite successful. The older brothers have also been quite successful in businesses similar to the father's. It seems the client was the 'black sheep' of the family in that he was not as successful and the father was quite critical of him throughout childhood and early adolescence. His father used to tell him that he'd never be as successful as his older brothers.

It appears the client took this as a challenge and worked very hard in high school, excelled in academics and athletics . . . and his business career up until lately. The wife indicated that he is a pure "workaholic" and never hesitated to bring work home or work on vacations. She said she has never seen him take more than one day off for full relaxation in their ten years of marriage. They have three children, but he never has spent any time with them, preferring to work. She reported some marital conflict stemming from his workaholic lifestyle, complaining that she had often fought with him about the need to have some attention for herself and for the children.

[Psychiatrist]: Yes, the mental status showed there were no abnormalities in the sensorium, no psychotic thinking or experiences, no gross distortions of reality, and in short, I believe the major difficulty is a 'hypomanic personality,' demonstrated by the workaholic lifestyle the social worker detailed. When I spoke with the client, he had pressure of speech and was most concerned about how long treatment would take, how soon he would be released, because he stated that he had very pressing business matters to attend to, mentioning some big business deals, apparently to impress me. Behind all the bluster, he seemed to have a strong sense of inferiority, which he was constantly talking to cover up, mentioning his business exploits, all the powerful businessmen he knew and so on.

[Psychologist]: The psychological test data tends to confirm the same. This is a person who has Denial Personality Disorder/Traits. He is likely to deny emotional problems, and to use impulsive acting-out behaviors to relieve emotional distress when it builds up. He has a high energy level and is likely to engage in a very busy external life, partly as a defense against dealing with internal emotional problems. If he is stressed here in the program, he might impulsively leave or opt out. On the other hand, it is going to take some strong confrontation to break through the denial and defensiveness which is hurting him now.

[Nurse]: Yes, I noticed the same traits that you all have mentioned. He has come to the nursing station several times each day and started conversations which seem designed to impress us with his business achievements. Lately he has been having what appears to be a 'flight into health.' He talks about how he was bothered by this and bothered by that, but that now he's overcome all these problems and thinks he's ready to leave the hospital and return to work.

[Counselor]: One thing we can certainly expect in group is the denial of all emotional problems and a probable focus on his business career, putting his career in the best possible light to cover up his personal problems. If this happens, we may have to step in and help prod the group to confront him. This is a new group and they may be hesitant to confront him very strongly on their own. We might also assess how the client is feeling after feedback because we want to make sure that he doesn't leave treatment impulsively after the group session.

[Social Worker]: On the other hand, let's make the intervention as nonintrusive as possible. I think this group's beginning to take more responsibility. Perhaps if the presentation goes as we suspect, we can just stop the group and ask them to provide feedback to the presenter about whether he's giving them material that they'll be able to give feedback on later. This minimal sort of intervention might be just enough to get them going on the right track of taking responsibility for the group processes.

[Nurse]:   I agree. I talked with Mr. A___ [one of the more assertive group members] yesterday and he said he was going to start interrupting presentations whenever they are superficial.

[Psychiatrist]:   Yes, I agree with that overall approach. Yesterday the group members stopped asking questions of their own accord and I think they're ready to take another step in assuming more responsibility for the group. So go ahead with this plan.

MAXIMIZE GROUP RESPONSIBILITY

There are several group management guidelines for the presentation stage. The first is to *always let the group do as much as it is capable of doing.* For instance, if the group seems to be gradually moving toward more and more emotional handling of the material, then it's best to keep "hands off" if possible. On the other hand, if presentations are repeatedly factual, boring, and showing none of the emotional life of the presenter, then it's time for the staff to stop a presentation and ask the group "what's going on?" For instance:

[Mr. J.]:   When I got in the army, we went to the Philippines for a short assignment and I was the army secretary. We were doing reconnaissance for the military and I had to write one report after another about the plane flights going out across the Pacific. Another of my duties was to drive the colonel's private car. The colonel and I got along real well and we used to go out sometimes and do some drinking. The colonel was a swell guy and I'll never forget him. He taught me how to do things the right way in the military. When I came back to the states, the colonel and I remained friends and I developed a good correspondence with him. He's been dead some years now, but I still think fondly of him every now and then and of all the good times we used to have in the service . . . [continues this long and dry monologue] . . .

[Reactions]: Several people in the group are fidgeting very noticeably. People begin to walk in and out of the group. Several group members are yawning repeatedly. One of the group members has gone to sleep and is snoring quietly in the corner.

[Therapist]: [Interrupting the presentation] What's going on here today? [Group members are silent and look around as if they don't know].

[Therapist]: What I am talking about is that several of you appear restless, fidgeting. People are getting up and going to the bathroom. Several of you are yawning and one has fallen asleep. What's going on?

[Ms. H.]: This presentation's very boring. I hate to say that, but I don't think I'm the only one who thinks so. Mr. J.'s not telling us anything about himself. He's just telling 'war stories' about being in the service.

[Mr. B.]: I thought I was the only one bored, but I guess not. I was bored and felt myself getting sleepy, but I didn't know what to do. I still don't know what to do. I was thinking of leaving the room and not coming back but I was afraid I would get in trouble and be discharged from treatment.

[Therapist]: So what can we do when this happens? [Group Silence]

[Therapist]: One thing you could do is what I just did. Stop the group and find out what is going on. If you feel that

the presentation is not going anywhere, then you
could stop the presenter and give him feedback. Tell
him what he needs to begin talking about in order for
you to have some productive feedback for him later.

Note that the therapist initially made a very non-
directive intervention: "What's going on in group today?"
When that didn't work, the therapist became more specific
in pointing out the symptoms of the problem: fidgeting
and yawning. This intervention led the group to a discussion pointing out that they were ignoring their feelings of
boredom and the perception that the presentation was
fairly meaningless, at least in terms of their being able to
give feedback about it later. The staff went on to explore
the possible reasons for the group's failure to take the
initiative in confronting the defenses and denial of the
presenter.

INTERVENTIONS: LESS IS MORE!

Always intervene in such a way as to prevent or mini-
mize the need for similar interventions. "Why did we have
to stop the presenter? Why didn't one of you speak up and
tell the presenter that he wasn't dealing with the kind of
emotional material we need in order to provide good
feedback?" This is a very important principle. If it is not
practiced, then the group will become dependent upon the
therapist to tell the presenter that he needs to offer more
emotional feelings and material.

[Howie]:   I've told you all about myself. What's your feedback?

[Ms. S.]: I think you ought to move out of your parents' house. They've always treated you bad. That's your main problem. You ought to solve it by moving out and then going to N.A. meetings regularly.

[Howie]: But, right now I don't have the money to move out. So I'll probably just stay with them a few more weeks until I can get a job.

[Mr. D.]: I think you ought to move out now. Don't wait another two weeks. Your parents are just causing you one problem after another and it's not fair to you. You could go to a halfway house if you don't have anywhere to stay and they could probably refer you to an employment service.

[Howie]: I tried to stay in a halfway house before and it just didn't work. I don't get along living with a bunch of people. I still think the best thing for me to do is to stay with my parents for the next couple of weeks and then move out when I get a job.

[Mr. D.]: Maybe you could get a job while you're in the treatment center here and then you could get a loan from someone and start out in your own apartment or duplex. That would solve the problem of your not wanting to live with other people.

[Howie]: But, the counselors already told me that I have to wait until the third week of the program to talk with a jobs counselor. I'm supposed to focus on myself until then.

[Therapist]: What's going on in the group today?

[Ms. W.]: We're giving Howie advice instead of feedback. Also, Howie is defending himself and responding to the advice.

[Ms. C.]: We're not really telling Howie anything about himself. We're just telling him what to do. And he doesn't even accept that. By trying to solve his problems, he can just say 'Well, I tried that before and it doesn't work' and then put the responsibility right back on us for finding a different solution. I think he's too dependent.

[Therapist]: Talk directly to Howie.

[Ms. C.]: [continuing] Yeah, I think you're too dependent . . . blaming your parents for your problems and setting up the group to blame your parents. Because they feel you are too dependent, they're trying to tell you what to do, instead of telling you how you could grow as a person. Also, I think you're fooling yourself about going back to your parents for a couple of weeks. Once you're back with them, you'll be blaming them again and before you know it, you'll be 'using' again. I don't blame them for some of the things they've done—they're probably trying to help you to become independent and get out on your own. Your parents are not the problem. They're not here in the treatment center. You have the problem! You stay with them because you're afraid or too irresponsible to get out on your own and take care of yourself. All the advice in the world won't get you to grow up and take responsibility if you don't decide to do this yourself.

[Mr. T.]: I agree with that and, also, once the group started giving you advice, you started playing 'Yes, but,' giving the group all kinds of reasons why you couldn't follow our advice. That shows you were just playing a game with us, so we would get hung up on advice instead of giving you feedback about yourself.

[Other group members now see what is happening and begin to give more productive feedback instead of advice. At the end of the group session, the therapist asks the group a question.]

[Therapist]: Let's finish with Howie's situation and talk about what happened in group today. The group got sort of side-tracked in giving advice and we had to intervene. Some group members were aware of what was happening, but you waited for the staff to intervene. Why?

[Ms. W.]: I could have said something because I was very aware of what was happening. But I felt sorry for Howie and I didn't want to say anything to hurt his feelings . . . even though I know I should have said something. After thinking about it, I know a lot of advice won't help him, so from now on I'm just going to say whatever I think I need to say.

[Several group members echo these sentiments].

[Ms. C.]: I think Howie made a presentation which made us all feel sort of sorry for him. So then we wanted to blame others for his problems and wanted to give him advice. We didn't want to confront him with his behavior. Next time when I am feeling sorry for someone, I'll give them this feedback so they can know they're seeing themselves as a victim.

[Therapist]: Yes, whenever you have any feelings in regard to the presenter, it's better to tell the presenter what those feelings are than to react to them yourself. For example, it is better to tell the presenter that you feel sorry for him because he is presenting himself as a victim, than to start fixing him and giving him advice about what to do.

INTERPRETING BEHAVIOR

The therapist should avoid interpreting behavior unless it is absolutely necessary or unless group members have exhausted their interpretive feedback. It is always tempting to provide interpretations, but if the staff interprets early, then the clients will tend to depend upon the staff for interpretations and will not assert their own ideas. If therapist interpretations seem necessary, it is usually best to wait until the end of the group session to give them. If a group is working effectively, the therapist's interpretive feedback probably will be nothing more than a repetition of the group's feedback, with perhaps a little more clarification. In some cases, the therapist may want to talk privately with the presenter after the rest of the group has broken up. This technique has the advantage of making the group members even more independent and responsible, because then they have no direct knowledge of what the therapist said and therefore cannot be influenced by it.

PROMPTING FEEDBACK

Another function of therapist feedback is to prod, elicit, and encourage. For example, the group may be giving feedback, but several members remain passive, saying nothing. The following illustrates what a therapist does in response to this:

[During the Feedback Phase, Mr. R., Mr. D., and Mrs. G. have not given feedback even though group time is about up. Mr. R. and Mrs. G. seem very uncomfortable, squirming in their seats and sighing.]

[Therapist]:   We hope that everyone will join in and give feedback because this has been a very good presentation by Lloyd.

[Several minutes pass. Others continue to give feedback while Mr. R., Mr. D. and Mrs. G. remain silent.]

[Therapist]:   Who have we not heard from in the group?

[Mr. R.]:   I don't have anything to say that hasn't been said already. There's no need to repeat what's already been said by others.

[Therapist]:   But it is important to repeat feedback. That alone gives it power. And it's important for Lloyd to find out what you think about his situation. So why don't you go ahead and try it in your own words.

[Mr. R.]:   Okay. Lloyd, I agree with the group that you don't know your own limits. You seem to think that other people ought to do just what you think they should do and when they don't, then you get mad. You got mad at me when we were partners in that bridge game the other day. I didn't play like you thought I ought to. Since then, I've just felt like steering clear of you.

[Mr. D.]:   You and I are roommates and I didn't really want to tell you anything because I have to live with you. I don't want any repercussions, but I guess I'll have to tell you anyway. I've noticed you're automatically 'bossy' in anything that comes up. When your wife was visiting, and you were telling her to do this and do that and so

	on . . . very pushy. I could see that she didn't want to do some of those things, but was afraid to say 'no.'
[Mrs. G.]:	I can't think of anything to say to Lloyd.
[Therapist]:	You mean that you've been living with Lloyd here at the treatment center for over two weeks and you just heard this presentation and you don't have anything to say?
[Mrs. G.]:	Let me think about it for a while. [Some group laughter here.]
[Therapist]:	Remember, we expect you to give feedback during each group session. Tomorrow, we want you to be prepared to give some good feedback to the presenter. If everyone said that they had nothing to say, then there would be no feedback at all. Think about it. This group is your responsibility, too.

Notice that in the above example, the staff tried the most general approach first, and slowly focused more and more upon individual group members when the general prompting did not work. This is a related principle of intervention: *start with the most general and low-level intervention and gradually proceed to the more powerful and specific, stopping at whatever level appears to work.*

RESISTANCE TO FEEDBACK

Therapists conducting group psychotherapy with addicts must often deal with client resistance to feedback. This resistance often involves the client's trying to "answer" the feedback, providing reasons or justifications for everything. Another form of resistance is talking at length any time feedback is received. Sometimes the client dilutes the feedback by accepting it and then qualifying. Consider the following example:

[Lloyd]: That's all there is.

[Ms. B.]: I think you ought to move out on your own. You're too dependent on your elderly mother and she's enabling your drug use.

[Lloyd]: But I can't leave my mother alone at her age and none of my brothers or sisters will move in with her 'cause they're all married and live in other states. So, I have to stay with her.

[Mr. D.]: I think you need your mother, not the other way around. You've been in this program for over three weeks and she seems to be doing okay. She looked pretty good when she came to visit you.

[Lloyd]: Yeah, but you don't know what she has to put up with at home. She has to shop, cook, and clean up all by herself. I just can't let her do that. Besides, I can stop drinking on my own and I intend to. Anyway, my mother hates drinking with a passion.

[Therapist]: Lloyd, why don't you just listen for a while and not respond. You're blocking the feedback before you really have a chance to think about it. Just listen to the feedback and think about it for a few days. Then, if you decide it really doesn't apply, you can dismiss it. But first, try to listen to what the group is telling you.

This intervention by the therapist was to help the client accept valuable feedback from the group. With an extremely resistant client, this kind of intervention may have to be repeated several times.

EVALUATING THE GROUP SESSION

The aim of group psychotherapy is to promote the growth of individual members, but this is dependent upon the adequacy of the group process. The therapist should reserve the final fifteen minutes of the group session for a discussion and evaluation of the group process, shaping and redirecting it as necessary.

[Therapist]:   Neil has received a lot of good feedback and I hope that throughout the day and the rest of the program, you'll continue to try to get feedback from the people in group. And I hope they'll continue to give it. How do you feel about the feedback you received?

[Neil]:   I think the feedback has been excellent. I was aware of some of these things before, but I had always kidded myself that it really wasn't true. I needed to hear it real strong like I did today in group.

[Therapist]:   Good. Now let's move on and talk for a moment about how the group went today. How do you all think the group went?

[Ms. H.]:   I think the group is going fairly well, but I do want to say something about what is happening. The same four people are carrying the group and the rest of the group is simply following the lead of those four people. Jason and Dick are always the last to give feedback and usually repeat what's already been said. I think they're playing it safe.

[Jason]: I tell you, there's several in here who run their mouth the whole time so nobody else can get a word in edgewise. And then, at the end when you can say something, everything has already been said.

[Ms. H.]: There's a simple solution to that. Tomorrow you be the first one to give feedback. Just jump in there and give the feedback first and then you won't have to repeat somebody else's.

[Jason]: But I need time to think about what I want to say. [Laughter by the group.]

[Ms. H.]: I think that's a lot of bull. You're passive here and outside both. I don't think that's bad, but I think that's what keeps you from saying something until the very end. I think you're a little scared to risk your own opinion until the group is somewhat committed to something.

[Jason]: Yeah, but whenever I start to say something Mr. F. cuts me off. He dominates this group anyway. It makes me angry and I figure that if he's so smart, just let him run the damn group and take the responsibility for it.

[Mr. F.]: So that's it! I knew there was something since the first time we were in group together—I knew that you had something against me. I didn't know you felt inferior, though, and that you resented me talking out. I really haven't meant to offend you and I hope we can work out this problem.

[Jason]: Well, you're my roommate and I haven't wanted to tell you. But every time we start talking you always interrupt me, and then I say, well 'what the hell,' why should I talk, and I feel very angry.

[Mr. F.]:   I really didn't realize that I was upsetting you. I'm sorry if I did. Let's try to straighten this out, because I don't want to be your roommate and have you feeling angry at me.

[Therapist]:   We're running out of time. Jason, will you try to work on speaking out earlier in the group and becoming more involved in the feedback and continue to work on this situation with your roommate?

[Jason]:   Yes, I will.

[Therapist]:   Now let's talk with some others who are sort of quiet.

In the example above, the group members processed the problems going on in group rather adequately, and the therapist played only a minor role. However, this won't always be the case, as the following example shows:

[The group ends with feedback completely exhausted, but about 15 minutes earlier than usual.]

[Therapist]:   How did the group go today?

[Mr. R.]:   I think the group went very well today. I didn't see anything wrong with it at all.

[Mr. L.]:   I agree. I think everyone worked real hard and that the group did a good job.

[Mr. P.]:   I spoke out early today and other people had to repeat my feedback, instead of the other way around, like it usually is.

[Long dead silence]

[Therapist]: What about the fact that we have finished group all this week about fifteen or twenty minutes ahead of schedule?

[Mr. C.]: Maybe we're working well together . . . very efficiently.

[Mr. R.]: Why should we prolong this and 'beat a dead horse?'

[Long dead silence]

[Therapist]: I think I have to give the group feedback based upon my experience and I hope you'll trust that experience. Most groups we have here not only take up the whole time period, they usually go over the time period and the staff usually has to stop the group so the clients can go on to the next activity. I also notice that here the group members usually give one piece of feedback and then 'shut down.' There isn't much spontaneity. You've made a good start as a beginning group. What I'm indicating is that you can get a lot more involved and take the issues to a deeper level. You're all going to benefit from that. I hope that all of you will give more than one piece of feedback. You don't have to give it all at once. Give some feedback, let others give some, and then take what has been said further. If we're really working well, the staff will almost always have to stop the group process. It won't stop by itself. Will you please think about that? [Several group members nod in agreement]. Okay, that's it for today.

Here the therapist had to give the group members the benefit of group comparisons, which would have been impossible for them to be aware of since they don't get to see how other groups function. It is important to deliver such feedback in a kind and noncritical way, simply to demonstrate the point that the group could carry the discussion further and become more intensively involved in the feedback process.

ASSESSING GROUP DYNAMICS

In all the group management principles explained so far, it has been implicit that the therapist detect or assess what is happening in the group at any time in order to make the appropriate intervention or to know when to make an intervention. Often our task is simply to assess the behavior of the group and bring this behavior into consciousness; in other words, make the group more aware of what is going on so that they can bring about changes that they feel are needed. This assessment can be a difficult task, but one that I think can be achieved by following a few simple principles.

Body Language. Assess the general "feel" of the group during the presentation and feedback periods by carefully observing the body language of the group. What are the facial expressions of the presenter and the rest of the group? Does everyone seem attentive, for example, changing facial expressions in response to the changing tenor of the presentation; or are peoples' expressions "flat," "frozen," or "blank" as if they are perhaps hiding their emotions? Are people sitting with their arms and legs crossed, perhaps indicating a closed and defensive posture, or are they relaxed and open to what is happening? When the presenter receives some uncomfortable feedback, does he flush and clench his fists in a show of anger, or does he try to assume a receptive posture and reflect carefully upon what he is hearing? Examine the following situation:

[Nelson]: Look [clenching fists], I told you [to Jeanne] that I wasn't afraid of my wife getting a job and making as much money as I do [face flushes and veins on forehead protrude].

[Long silence]

[Therapist]: Nelson, you seem to have some feelings about that . . . and your interaction just now with Jeanne. Would you like to receive some feedback from the group on that point?

[Nelson]: No, not particularly.

[Mr. G.]: I'd like to give you some feedback anyway. You responded to Jeanne's feedback very defensively, clenching your fists and flushing. That makes me think you're angry about the feedback and that maybe there's something to it.

[Nelson]: Look, I know what I do and don't do . . . or feel.

[Therapist]: Maybe you ought to give the feedback a chance— you seem to be getting rid of it right away. Later, after you've thought about the feedback, you may still want to get rid of it, but for right now, it might be worthwhile to think about it.

[Nelson]: I'll try. But I just don't like this kind of feedback.

Here, a group member actually helped the presenter become aware of something he wasn't in touch with. This is a large part of improving the group functioning: bringing the nonverbal into verbal awareness.

Emotional Climate. Assess the emotional climate of the group. Are group members reacting spontaneously, or are they going through the motions in an apparent attempt to satisfy the therapist? If they are reacting spontaneously, they will react emotionally and express appropriate feelings in the group when the situation calls for it. Do they stop a boring presentation and let the presenter know what they need to hear? Do they interrupt and ask for clarification when the presenter skips over an obviously very emotionally-laden episode in his life?

[Mr. G.]: I came back from my trip early and I found my wife in bed with my best friend. I just stood there and was frozen——they froze too. I thought for a while about getting my gun and then killing them, but I just stood there a while and then left. Later, I moved to Tennessee and got divorce papers from my wife, who had also sued me for custody of my three kids. Hell, I decided I just wouldn't fight it and signed the papers and sent them to her the same day . . . [Long pause] . . . Later, I got married to a woman in Mississippi and we got along real good . . . [continues with story].

In this illustration, group members suppressed their feelings instead of acting on them. They allowed the presenter to skip over an emotionally-laden episode—when he was angry enough to kill but completely stifled his feelings. The therapist could do several things in this situation. He could stop the presentation and point out that there seem to be some strong feelings which are not being discussed. Or, he could wait till the group process evaluation at the close of the session and point out that the group had allowed the presenter to skip over some very important material. In either case, there needs to be some discussion of why the group allowed the presenter to avoid talking about what must have been very powerful emotions emerging from the adultery incident. Again, the point of the intervention is to highlight what is happening, in this case avoidance by the presenter and group, and to encourage facing situations and dealing with them.

On-task Behaviors. Assess the behavior of the group in response to the task. Do they fall asleep or repeatedly leave the room during the presentation? Do they stare out the window or pick up a newspaper? Do they begin to write letters?

[Carol]: That's my childhood. When I was about fifteen I started to work on my own. I just couldn't stand the boredom of school and so I became a secretary . . . [Pete falls asleep and starts snoring heavily until awakened by a group member] . . . as I was saying . . .

[Therapist]: [Interrupting] Carol, why don't you tell Pete how you feel about his falling asleep during your presentation.

[Carol]: It has made me a little angry——on top of feeling nervous.

[Pete]: I just thought the presentation was a little boring and I felt sort of sleepy and closed my eyes for a minute to rest them and just fell asleep. I wasn't trying to aggravate you.

[Therapist]: What could you have done instead of fall asleep, Pete?

[Pete]: I know if we get bored, we're supposed to tell the presenter . . . but I knew she was holding back. She told

me the other day that there were a bunch of things that
she couldn't tell and she wasn't going to tell.

[Mr. C.]: I guess I'm partly responsible, too. I didn't say anything
because I was just daydreaming about what I was going
to do this weekend.

[Therapist]:   Maybe in the future, if the presentation is making
you fall asleep, it would be better to go ahead and
confront the presenter.

In the above example, the intervention helped the
group members look at their behaviors and translate these
"acting-out" behaviors into verbal/social problem-solving
approaches.

Energy Level. Assess the energy level of the group. Do
we have to repeatedly prompt the group to continue
because the members fall silent again and again during the
session? Or, is the energy level so high that we have to
often intervene to settle down members who become too
agitated?

[Phil]: I thought I gave a pretty good presentation, but I haven't
received much feedback. How come?

[Long silence]

[Therapist]:   I agree with Phil. It appears that something is going
on in the group and it needs to be discussed.

[Mr. H.]: To be honest, probably most of us don't feel like doing
this today. There's a lot of feelings about the way Harry
M____ was discharged last night and there's been lots
of talk about it.

[Therapist]: Maybe we'd better stop the feedback and talk about what's going on in the group. Is that okay with you, Phil?

[Phil]: Yeah. I'd still like to get some feedback though.

[Therapist]: Fair enough. Now let's hear from the group. Do all of you have feelings about Harry M____'s discharge?

[Mr. W.]: I think we're all angry about it for one thing. Harry told us you'd done a lot of drug screens on him and then discharged him after one positive drug screen. We've read that those tests are not very reliable. And Harry told us that he hadn't been using any cocaine at all. He claimed the staff just didn't like him and had been looking for reasons to discharge him. We think that's unfair and we just don't feel like working very hard today.

[Mr. G.]: I for one think it's a raw deal and that the staff is really being crummy about the whole thing.

[Therapist]: Let me explain a little bit about the drug testing we do here. We have been very concerned about the drug testing and in fact, we used to require two 'positives' before we discharged anyone. Of course, this was quite a problem sometimes, because the drug testing for two positives could take up to 10 days. When that happened, and the client was in fact using drugs, then the nonusing clients here were subjected to ten days of someone using drugs right under their noses.

During the past two years, drug testing has improved and the laboratory now tells us that they can be more than ninety-nine percent positive about drug use when a client gets a 'strong positive.' They still test the sample twice. Both tests have to be strongly positive for the client to be discharged. Remember, part of our responsibility to you is to provide you with a drug-free environment while you're here. And we take this responsibility seriously.

[Mr. W.]:   That's different from what I thought. Like I said, Harry told us there was only one test and that the testing was sloppy.

[Mr. G.]:   I guess we should have asked you at the beginning of group, like you've told us to do whenever there's really something going on that we need to know about.

[Therapist]:   A good point——there's no reason why you can't ask about something you're concerned about. If someone has a problem and doesn't work it out, then the group won't have the concentration to really help the presenter. That's what happened today. The group simply didn't have its mind on Phil's presentation and the feedback sort of 'stalled' and didn't go anywhere. I think that since our time is almost up, the best thing to do is to take a break and then continue tomorrow and let Phil re-present.

[Several group members agree].

The group's low energy level, particularly in contrast to the energy level of previous sessions, was a sign that something was going wrong in the group; the problem needed to be brought to consciousness and talked about. The point of the intervention was to bring up the problem indicated by the energy level and use verbal/social problem solving to deal with it.

Group Cohesiveness. Assess the group's cohesion and the dominant way in which people interact. The therapist should be especially alert for signs of covert hostility, various subgroupings that form, competition for control of the group, vindictiveness, and threatening behaviors.

[Mr. G.]: Larry [presenter], I like you but I have to be honest. You're winding up in prison after prison. You just got out of jail and it won't be long before you'll be back, if you keep up what you're doing. You say you don't like jail, but then you always wind up back in there. That makes me think maybe you really like it for some reason. Maybe its comfortable . . . always plenty of structure and you have someone to tell you what to do day and night so you never have to be responsible or make decisions on your own. I don't want to hurt you, but think you ought to think about these possibilities.

[Mr. P.]: I feel the same way, Larry. You're very likeable and by the way you act around here, it's hard to believe you've been in all the jails you talk about. Yes, there's something about jail that you like or you wouldn't keep going there. I remember you even said that lately you haven't even tried to cover up your crimes. It's as if you want to get caught. Maybe you want to get rid of your freedom so you won't have to make any choices in your life.

Assuming that the nonverbal signals aren't inconsistent, the above example shows that there is good feeling among these three group members and that Mr. P____ and Mr. G____ really care about Larry. This caring attitude, which was clearly communicated, will really empower the ensuing feedback, because even if the feedback is critical and hurts, the presenter acknowledges it more fully. He knows that the people giving it really care about him and that the thoughts and feelings are genuine.

The ultimate purpose of assessment is to identify group trends which might become problematic trends and to confront them, encouraging the use of verbal/social problem-solving to deal with them. A lone therapist or counselor cannot monitor simultaneously all the behaviors noted above; this is one reason why it is important for more than one staff member to be present during the group session.

What is the "norm" of a really well-functioning group? In my opinion, you will be able to spot a well-functioning group because it will have a high energy level without any impulsive acting out. The group will have free-flowing, spontaneous interactions, a feeling of goodwill among the members, and a sense that they are generally cooperative and working on the common goal of providing constructive and honest feedback for each other.

8

Common Problems
CORRECTIVE TECHNIQUES

The examples of group interaction in previous chapters have demonstrated several common problems a therapist can expect to encounter in group therapy with addicts. These can be categorized as "presentation," "feedback," or "process" problems. These common problems will be summarized in this chapter along with techniques that can be helpful in correcting them.

PRESENTATION PHASE PROBLEMS

Premature presentations. These usually appear as "overzealousness" on the part of the client. For example, a client may have just joined the group and yet he wants to be the first to present. Usually this individual feels quite anxious and wants to "get the presentation over with, so that he can relax." Or, in the case of an antisocial personality, he may quickly realize that it is best to present early, before the group becomes sophisticated enough to realize that he may be manipulating them. It would be a bad idea for either the overly anxious or antisocial member to present prematurely since it would be of little or no benefit to him. It is much better to let this person's anxiety build while the group matures.

Superficial presentations. Often, addicted persons will present almost completely factual self-disclosures, devoid of feelings or emotional content. They may focus on very superficial aspects of their lives and discuss them at great length. For example, an army veteran may avoid emotional content by describing in great detail how combat operations were performed in Viet Nam. Straight factual presentations don't engage group members emotionally and present little opportunity for productive feedback. During such presentations, the group may become listless; if the problem isn't verbalized, acting-out behaviors may appear, such as fidgeting, nodding or actually falling asleep, leaving the room for coffee, or asking for permission to go to the rest room. Therapists must let feelings of discomfort build enough to provide strong motivation for appropriate feedback. But you must be careful. There is a delicate point at which the group members may get so "turned off" that they simply don't care.

If the group doesn't intervene after about fifteen minutes of a superficial presentation, and there are clear signs of acting out, then the therapist should say something like, "Let's stop for a minute. Are you all getting the kind of information you need in order to give feedback later?" Or, "Let's stop for a minute. How are you all feeling?" (and if this doesn't get a response) "Mr. Smith, I noticed you seem quite sleepy. Is it the presentation that's causing this?" In other words, the therapist would move from asking for a general response to pointing out more specific behaviors if the first question is not productive. If this sort of intervention is timed correctly, several of the group members will give the feedback that the presenter is not really giving any useful information; they might even go so far as to say that they're bored or sleepy. It would also be helpful at this point to encourage the group members to tell the presenter exactly what information they need, if they do not provide this feedback spontaneously. As always, it would be helpful for the therapist to explore why the group members did not spontaneously stop the presentation themselves, so that the staff had to intervene in the process.

Terse presentations. The same general approach applies to another frequently encountered problem, the presentation which is too brief. Many clients will give a very brief presentation, no longer than five to fifteen minutes, ending with the "classic" statement, "Well, I haven't had much happen to me in my life," notwithstanding the fact that the person is 65 years old. Usually, it is a mistake to move into the feedback stage in such an instance; rather, it is best to let the group indicate whether or not they received enough information to prompt useful feedback. One option, at this point, is to ask the client to repeat parts of the presentation, but with more detail and depth. Or, the therapist may conclude that the client is not interested in feedback and end the group early.

Terminating the group discussion can motivate some clients who are simply going through the motions of getting treatment to satisfy an employer or spouse. Ending the group early is analogous to discharging such an unmotivated client from treatment early. It is a clear message to the addict that he has not yet entered real treatment, and helps him avoid embracing the delusion that he has had treatment, when actually all that he has done is perfunctorily fulfill mechanical requirements. This is an important point, because many addicts continue denial throughout treatment, going through the motions and then deluding themselves that they are "cured." This sets the person up for a later relapse. When addicts are obviously not working in group, it is important to give them clear messages about their resistance.

"Beat-the-clock." In extreme contrast to the terse presentation, clients often play "beat the clock." They go on and on (sometimes telling very fascinating and interesting stories) and end up filling the entire hour-and-a-half session. Then there is no time for feedback, which must be postponed until the next session. Often, such a client is actually dodging feedback; he is taking up all the time talking in hopes that any feedback will be short and superficial. Also, feedback given the next day, or later, will often be "cold" and less effective because many clients will have forgotten much of the presentation. If the presentation has already gone on for thirty-five or forty minutes, is nowhere near ending, and no one in the group has said anything about it, then the therapist should prompt the presenter to conclude within the next few minutes. Sometimes the client is so resistive that even this does not work. The therapist should then arbitrarily stop the presenter to ensure adequate time for the group members to provide feedback. In such cases, it is hoped that the group will point out the client's resistance to feedback. At any rate, the group members will have to provide feedback only on the part of the presentation they have heard; however, in a great majority of those cases, such feedback will be as good as if they had heard the whole presentation. This is much preferable to endorsing the game of avoidance.

FEEDBACK PHASE PROBLEMS

Rescuing. Often, a client who rescues another from the feedback consequences of a presentation will himself tend to avoid dealing with the consequences of his own behavior and unpleasant emotions. In essence, he will be performing the service that he wants to have performed for him when the time for his presentation comes. If rescuing continues for awhile without group members intervening, the therapist should point out what is happening and confront the rescuer. The staff might follow up the confrontation of rescuing with a question to the whole group about why they didn't say anything about the rescue attempt.

Passivity. Passivity is the repeated pattern, by one or more group members, of failing to give feedback. After the passive group member has been given ample time to improve his performance, and if the group itself does not confront the issue, then the therapist may need to ask directly for feedback. For example, suppose that the presenter has been receiving a good deal of feedback from several of the group members and the passive group member still hasn't said anything. The therapist might say something like, "Mr. Jones, what do you think about the situation? Can you tell the presenter what you see going on with him?" Another general technique is to meet in private with the passive group member. Let him know what the expectations are and that he is not meeting those expectations. The therapist might say, "Mr. Jones, we expect you to give feedback during every group session and you haven't been. Is there anything we can do to help you? What seems to be stopping you?" At this point, the therapist could explore the client's resistance and perhaps help him deal with it. Leave the client with the firm expectation of having to give feedback during the next session, and that you will be observing this carefully.

Hostile or Aggressive Feedback. Group members sometimes mistake a harsh tone for the best tone with which to give feedback. They proceed to give feedback in a harsh and aggressive manner, which is perceived by others as a "shredding" of the presenter. Again, it is hoped that the group members will respond to this situation, but if they do not, then the therapist needs to move in rather quickly and point out the aggressiveness of the feedback. The therapist could make clear the expectation that feedback be assertive and constructive in tone and manner, and perhaps explore why the client is feeling the need to be hostile and aggressive. For example:

[Clifford]: Okay, that's it. I'm ready for the feedback.

[Harry]: Don't you see what the hell you're doing??? You're driving people away with your insolence and aggression——don't you have any better sense than that? What the hell do you think people will feel when you act like such an aggressive, hostile ass? You have all the finesse of a bull in a china shop. I'd sure hate to meet up with you in a bar.

[Therapist]: Harry, you seem to be very aggressive in your feedback. Can you tell us how you are feeling?

[Harry]: I guess I'm feeling okay, but this kind of upsets me sometime.

[Therapist]: I wonder if other group members can give Harry some feedback on how they saw him feeling just now.

[Clifford]: I thought he was feeling quite angry and I noticed his face, especially his ears, getting red. I also noticed his fists were clenched.

[Mr. D.]: Something I've noticed about Harry is that he is very similar to Clifford. I think he's sort of angry at himself and he sees himself in Clifford. These two seem to have a personality clash stronger than any others here. They're both very aggressive, controlling people.

[Mr. B.]: Yes, Harry and Clifford seem to want to control this group. They both want to be the leaders.

[Therapist]: What do you think of that Harry?

[Harry]: I never thought about it. I'm angry with myself and I do get aggressive sometimes. So does Clifford. Maybe there's something to it. I don't know. I'll just have to think it over for awhile. I didn't realize that I was getting that aggressive.

Often the aggressive client is angry at himself and projects this anger by providing very aggressive feedback to others. In such cases, aggressive clients usually act out against other aggressive clients. When this happens it is likely that rapid escalation, perhaps even to assaultive behavior, may occur. This situation can be very dangerous both for the group and for the individuals involved, as the following shows us:

[Clifford]: Okay, that's it. I'm ready for the feedback.

[Harry]: Don't you see what the hell you're doing? You're driving people away with your insolence and aggression——don't you have any better sense than that? What the hell do you think people will feel when you act like such an aggressive, hostile ass? You have all the finesse of a bull in a china shop. I'd sure hate to meet up with you in a bar.

[Clifford]: Look, you keep your mouth shut! I don't like that kind of language. Why don't you just keep your opinions to yourself. You're nothing but a junkie anyway—what do you know about alcoholism? All you junkies are trash. You don't even have enough sense to stay off drugs.

[Harry]: [Rising to his feet, pointing at Clifford and shaking his finger] Look, dirtbag, we can settle for once and for all who's trash and who's not. Just take a couple of steps over here and I'll rearrange your neurons . . .

[Clifford]: [Starts up out of his seat] . . .

[Therapist]: [Very firm, loud voice] Gentlemen, sit down at once! If you don't sit down, you'll have to leave the room. [Clifford refuses to sit down although Harry has re-seated himself]. Clifford, please leave the room. [Clifford complies and leaves the room]. Now, let's discuss what's happening here with the understanding that any further threats of violence will result in an immediate discharge.

[Mr. S.]: I've been seeing this coming all week. These guys are both very aggressive and angry. They're ready to take their anger out on the first guy who 'crosses' them. So they make targets for each other.

[Ms. A.]: They've been making nasty remarks about each other all week. Yes, they're a lot alike and they want to strike out at each other as a way of striking out at themselves. They've already created a lot of tension in the group.

[Ms. Y.]: This is probably the same kind of thing which happens to these guys on the outside. It's happening right here. Both these men have been in trouble with the law and everyone they know. They could learn something by working through these troubles. I think they should pledge to avoid any acting out and then get together and try to work out their differences. What do you think about that, Harry?

[Harry]: Well, I'd be willing to try it if Clifford will too. But if I'm attacked, I'll defend myself.

[Therapist]: That's reasonable enough, if we can get the same pledge from Clifford. I'd also like for both of you to commit to a 'no fault' interaction with each other; a commitment to not blame each other for how you are feeling when you interact. If you get to feeling bad, you'll just have to look to your own behavior for a source of relief.

[Harry]: That's okay by me, if Clifford will agree to do that.

[A team member leaves the group momentarily to find Clifford and secure the same pledge from him. Then both return.]

[Therapist]: How can we resolve this disagreement?

[Harry]: [to Clifford] I guess I was giving you some pretty rough feedback, at least that's what the group thinks. Also, I guess I feel some competition with you. I don't know quite how to handle that yet . . . I'll have to talk it out with you and the group. What do you say?

[Clifford]: I was feeling upset about the things I just talked about and maybe I overreacted to your feedback. I guess it was easier than really looking at how I was feeling about myself. I am willing to talk about this problem, because this seems to happen to me a lot. I get real angry and never solve anything . . . just walk off and never feel good about that person again. That's just no good.

It is very important for the therapist to act decisively whenever there is the possibility of aggressive acting out in the group. There is always the danger of bodily injury to the clients and irreparable harm to the group. Whenever there are signs of potential acting-out behaviors such as: 1) extreme agitation; 2) angry pointing of finger or fist at another group member; 3) standing up in a threatening way; 4) verbal threats of violence or bodily harm; or 5) walking threateningly toward another group member, the therapist must move quickly to bring the situation under control. Appropriate therapist actions include emphatically telling a client to stop threatening, to sit down, or to leave the room for a while until he feels under better control. The therapist may also dismiss the group in order to speak with a client alone. Be sure to attend to your own feelings during such episodes. If you fear that aggressive acting out is likely, then it probably is, and you should deal with it. After the episode has been brought under control and you feel that the clients are capable of processing the episode verbally, then do that.

Frequently, we find that the people who are prone to aggressive acting out in the group are very similar to each other; they hate themselves and project their self-hate onto the other person. In other words, they dislike in that person the same things they feel so badly about in themselves. If you can help them see this, it will help them move ahead in recovery. They will learn to "own" their problems and deal with themselves instead of focusing on other people. Successfully handling aggressive acting out in the group can provide a very good model of how verbal/social problem-solving skills are used.

Indirect feedback. Many clients will initially provide indirect feedback to the presenter. For example, someone may look out the window and say, "I think he (referring to the presenter) is too resentful to be happy." Such clients typically find it difficult to deal directly with others and attempt to talk "about" the presenter instead of "to" him. When this happens, the client should be encouraged to look the presenter in the eye and talk directly to him. Encourage the use of the phrase "I think you . . ." This fosters the skill of being able to deal directly with others in terms of one's own feelings.

GROUP PROCESS PROBLEMS

Failure to recognize problems. When a new group is formed, the therapist has an important educational function to perform. Group members must learn to recognize group process problems if the group is to become a powerful recovery mechanism. Early in the history of a group, the therapist should carefully note group process deficiencies and explore them with the group soon after they occur. The purpose of this is not only to learn to recognize common problems, but also to provide a model for group self-intervention.

[Mr. R.]: I'm through. So . . .?

[Mr. C.]: You were a football star in high school and college and that's part of the problem. You were used to everyone liking you, catering to you, and helping you get everything you want. It's too bad we do this to athletes. We put them on a pedestal and expect that they have perfect lives. But athletes are pressured all their lives to achieve this, achieve that.

[Ms. H.]:   Yeah, I agree that you became used to others taking care of you and pressuring you. Then you simply quit, moved away and didn't contact anyone for years until you got in trouble. Then you went back and tried to get the same people to enable and rescue you. You know, that's what usually happens to alcoholics and they know it. We all learned that the alcoholic game has several players: the alcoholic, the enabler, the rescuer, the victim, the persecutor. And sooner or later all alcoholics switch back and forth among some of these.

[During the group processing period after the end of the presentation]:

[Therapist]:   How did you think group went today?

[Mr. C.]:   I thought it went real well. There was plenty of feedback and we discussed some good points.

[Ms. H.]:   I thought the group went real well, too. I know that I did more talking than usual.

[After no complaints or problems are noted by the group]

[Therapist]:   I'd like to mention one problem I saw in the feedback today that you could become more aware of. That's the tendency to philosophize. For example, Mr. C___, you gave excellent feedback about the relationship between the presenter's early football career and his later dependency and demandingness. But then you started philosophizing about this country's tendency to expect a lot from athletes.

That weakens your feedback. The points that you
made are fascinating points, but we want to stick
strictly to what's happening with the presenter when
we are giving feedback, so that all the feedback is
a personal statement to him.

Often, instead of considering group process issues
when asked to, the group will continue to fixate on giving
the presenter feedback. Should this occur, the therapist
may have to repeatedly state that the work of the presenter is clearly ended and that we are now discussing how the
group is progressing and responding. This evasive action
by the group members is often evident when they are
resistant to looking at themselves and their behavior.

Overprocessing and focusing on externals. One of the
primary personality defenses of both the antisocial and
borderline personality disorder client is to "externalize"
conflicts. Externalizing sometimes involves creating conflicts between self and others to shift the focus off self
and onto others and their behavior. Many antisocial or
borderline clients will externalize by wanting to over-
process. They will interrupt the group process frequently
and attempt to start a group discussion about aspects of
the group process that are more their own individual
concern than the group's. This is usually very disruptive;
many times it is used to keep the group in disarray and to
distract it. Usually, the best strategy is to allow the group
enough time to focus on the disruptive individual and give
him feedback about his behavior, hoping for progress in
decreasing its frequency. However, if such domination
continues after a reasonable effort by the group, then the
therapist may be forced to conclude that the client is too
disruptive to work with in group therapy. In this case, it is

better to remove an "intractable" client from the group than to permit his continued involvement to prevent others from developing and the group as a whole from becoming a positive recovery force. This individual can be worked with individually and, later, reintegrated into that (or another) group.

9

The Working Cycle
FROM ADMISSION TO DISCHARGE

The working cycle of the therapy group can be divided into three distinct phases: beginning, middle, and transition-to-aftercare. These three cycles are clearly evident in inpatient programs, but less distinct in outpatient programs. Some outpatient groups have a high rate of daily turnover; new members must receive orientation and learn some of the basic requirements for participating effectively in group therapy. When there is an unstable pattern of group membership, the therapist must take a more active role in providing structure for the group than I have advocated here. For the most part, the following remarks pertain to the inpatient group, or the outpatient group which has a slow turnover in membership.

BEGINNING STAGE

During the *beginning stage*, group members will learn the fundamentals of how group therapy works and what their expectations should be. Much of the group work in the beginning stage is the development of an intellectual "game plan," which will be put into action later. Something to be aware of at this stage is that group members will often seem to have grasped more of the model than they actually understand. Their early understanding of group therapy is often superficial and primarily verbal. This is because the therapist is assuming most of the responsibility for conducting the beginning stage sessions. Only gradually are the clients asked to increase their participation and responsibility for the direction of the group. The structure and leadership provided by the therapist at this initial stage makes the clients comfortable, relaxed, and less anxious. For these reasons, the beginning stage of therapy is not distinguished by any intense problems for the therapist, unless a group has a high proportion of anti-social/borderline personalities who are prone to acting out their conflicting feelings. The previous chapter covered techniques for handling this kind of situation.

MIDDLE STAGE

This is the critical stage of a group's development, one which determines whether the group will become highly productive or bogged down in resistance and fear. During the middle phase, individual group members begin to present, and the rest of the group begins to provide feedback. This is an especially anxiety-arousing period, because the clients are slowly being "exposed"; any lack of trust among them can produce strong responses of fear and defensiveness. Although the presenter invariably begins to receive useful and stimulating feedback, it is nevertheless not something he really wants to hear or think about. In short, during the middle phase, the clients are beginning to face conflicts and inner feelings that are very disturbing. This is one of the reasons they haven't faced these conflicts before. If the lack of trust becomes too pronounced, then the group will invariably rebel against the whole process. The rebellion often takes the form of "externalizing," such as complaining about the staff, the program, the A.A. meetings, the rules about lunch, visitation—in short, about practically anything which can be complained about:

[Beginning of group]

[Therapist]:   It's time for Mr. B____ to present. Are we ready for that?

[Mr. D.]:   No, I want to bring up something beforehand that has been bothering me and I don't know what to do about it. On the night shift, the nurses are bossy and don't really treat us like we're adults. Last night, one of the nurses came in and turned off the TV and said we were goofing off and to 'get over to the A.A. Meeting right now.' So we were a little late. She didn't have to be like that. It bugs me. I think you ought to talk to these night nurses about that.

[Ms. R.]:   Oh yes, it happens all the time and I don't think you really know about it. It also happens during lunch. Whenever we ask for more food they say something like, 'That's all the doctor told me to give you—you're lucky to get that.' What can we do about that?

[Mr. M.]:   I agree. Also, the other day, we were supposed to have two activities and the staff was late for both of these activities. But if we're late, then some of the staff starts criticizing us for it and writes it down in our progress records.

[Therapist]:   Those points are very interesting, but I have also noticed that for the last three days in group, everyone is complaining about things going wrong in the program. And also, we spent the last two days talking about how you address problems in the program versus how you address problems in the group. What do you think is going on in the group?

[Mr. K.]:   Well, I guess we're talking about everything but what we are supposed to be. I get tired of hearing what's wrong with the program and what's wrong with the hospital. I just don't think that people in the group are ready to focus on themselves, so they're making other issues.

[Therapist]:   What do you see going on in the group that may be contributing to that sort of reaction? Is the group working well as a whole, and are there good relationships here?

[Long silence]

[Therapist]:   Well?

[Mr. Y.]:   I know one thing that's going on that's a problem: Danny's not really here to work on himself. He's told me that himself. And he talks and laughs about the presentations with some of the members of the other groups. I know one thing for sure—I'm not going to say anything in this group if he's in here. He'll make a big joke out of it and spread it all over the hospital.

[Mr. C.]: I've heard the same thing and I'm not saying anything either. The other thing is that the drug addicts and the alcoholics, as well as the blacks and whites, all get together and segregate. That's hurting the closeness of the group.

[Therapist]: Well, what do you have to say, Danny?

[Danny]: I honestly didn't know I couldn't ever talk about you guys outside of group. I didn't mention anyone's names, I was just talking about some of the things that happen to people, just like we alcoholics sometimes joke about how stupid we have been, when we get together in an A.A. meeting. I'm here to be serious——it is true that I first came in to convince my wife to take me back. But I've thought a lot about what I've heard here and now I realize that I have to do this for me. Doing it for anyone else is just a waste of time and fooling myself. I'm sorry about this and I won't say anything about the group outside anymore.

[Mr. W.]: That's an easy thing to say, but I don't know if I believe you. I would like to believe you, but I don't know if I can trust you again.

[Therapist]: Well, what would help us to trust Danny again——what concrete steps would we have to take to know that he is sincere?

[Ms. D.]: I think one thing would be for Danny to go ahead and make his first presentation to the group tomorrow. He hasn't presented yet and I think that his presentation would help us to know whether he is being sincere or not.

[Therapist]: Is that agreeable?

[All concur, including Danny]

[Therapist]: Alright, we mentioned earlier in our group orientation that we were going to have to avoid subgrouping
in order to help the group become unified and strong.
Apparently, there is a good deal of subgrouping going
on and its being done on 'drug of choice' and 'racial'
grounds. What can we do about this?

[Ms. C.]: I think that we just need to stop always pairing up with
the same people or group. All of us need to make an
effort to get to know each other much better so we can
learn from each other.

[The group continues to discuss these and other points that are
deterring them from becoming more involved in the actual work
of group therapy.]

On other occasions, the clients may appear to have
formed a "secret pact," wherein it appears that no one is
going to confront anyone so long as no one breaks the
pact. The presenters give one superficial presentation after
another, but no one confronts the presenter; no one gives
anything but superficial feedback. If this sort of resistance
continues for too long without being exposed and worked
on directly, the group may become frozen in a resistance
mode, particularly in a short inpatient rehabilitation
program. The reason is that when the transition-to-aftercare phase of the short program begins to loom, there is
a natural tendency for all groups to seek closure and "seal
off" the work they have done in an effort to gain a round-
ed sense of what they have accomplished.

These common threats to group progress make it
imperative for the staff to be especially alert during the
middle stage and to encourage group processing. In

situations involving constant group bickering and externalizing, or where there is one presentation after another with only superficial involvement and no honest or confronting feedback, the therapist may have to intervene. Presentations would be discontinued, and the group would spend from one to three group periods discussing "What's going on in group that we're not making progress or getting honest with each other?"

Almost always, there will be a "distrust" issue at the bottom of the resistance. But the therapist must get the group to admit it and to discuss and resolve it so that clients can go on to increase their honesty and openness with each other. On the other hand, we must remember that we are not miracle-workers, and that endless group processing sessions will not necessarily correct whatever communication problems exist. The group members themselves must be willing to examine these issues and change their behavior.

If strong group resistance continues throughout three consecutive group processing sessions, then it is probably better to return to individual presentations, working case by case toward improvement. The outlook for this kind of group is not good, though. Groups which cannot work through strong resistance during the latter part of the middle phase will, in my experience, remain stuck or frozen in the resistance phase. There will be only limited progress, if any.

At times, it seems as if the middle stage represents a "hump," which some groups are able to get over, and others are not, even with the best staff efforts to develop trust and overcome resistance. Once you have identified a group as being limited in its ability to increase intimacy and involvement among members, this doesn't mean you should abandon it. Continue working to increase honesty and intimacy, but, to lessen your own frustration, adjust your expectations of what can be accomplished.

TRANSITION-TO-AFTERCARE STAGE

During this phase, even the more successful group members begin to look toward discharge as the "ending" of therapy. Group members begin to seek "closure" or consolidation of their therapy experience. As they approach a discharge date, the members may present a second time, skipping a historical review and focusing directly on the issues that they now see as important to them, issues they anticipate as being crucial after their discharge from treatment:

[Mr. C.]: Well, I thought today that I would go over some of the feedback that I got on my first presentation. It was about how I have dealt with my anger toward my father. He put tremendous pressure upon me to be a big success and I apparently tried to please him. But I ended up having to use drugs and alcohol to handle all the pressure of the 'success trip.'

It's funny, but you know, as I have gotten nearer discharge I feel those same pressures again. Yesterday I started to think about what I needed to do after I return to my job, worrying about all the work I've missed and feeling like I will have to work double hard and put in overtime hours to make up the difference. Also, I put the same pressure on my recovery, trying to become the 'perfect recovering person,' doing the step-work perfectly and quickly——good grief! I found myself trying to get through all Twelve Steps before my discharge. The group mentioned this last night and after

> thinking about it, I could see how foolish it was to try that. But I just 'fall back' into those patterns so easily.

The above working session would represent a good continuation of the initial feedback session, with attention to the prevailing themes of the earlier work. Unfortunately, there is often a tendency to be less probing or introspective at this period. We must not mistake this as lessened involvement by clients in their treatment. It is a natural occurrence with any person who is trying to consolidate a period of experience and prepare to enter a new phase, a return to normal living experiences. Likewise, our clients will have a tendency to see themselves as resolving some conflicts and problems to a greater extent than is realistic.

We can do clients a service by pointing out that this is not the end of treatment, but the beginning of a recovery process which should continue for the rest of their lives. Sometimes it is a good idea to let the client present for the third time on the last day of his stay in an inpatient program to reinforce this point just before he is discharged. This is not to say that addicts should stay in group therapy for the rest of their lives. But it would certainly behoove them to continue in therapy for a year or longer and to continue working on the conflicts they have identified.

Toward this end, it is very important for the therapist and other professional staff to work jointly with clients on an appropriate discharge treatment plan. This should include providing guidance and referral to an outpatient psychotherapy group to continue the work that has already been accomplished. Such referral reinforces the perception that graduation from an inpatient program is not the end, but simply a transition, which is part of a continuing process. I would hope that every client who is discharged from an inpatient program has the name and address of a continuing psychotherapy group and an appointment for a first session there within a week's time. The discharged client should also have the name, address, and phone number of an A.A./N.A. meeting in his local area and a person who can act as a temporary contact or ride to the meeting. Follow-up appointments at the inpatient treatment institution for medications, (e.g. disulfiram) should be made. Also, the client should have the names, addresses, and phone numbers for Al-Anon, Nar-Anon, Ala-Teen and other appropriate family or codependent organizations. These, together, are the client's connection to continued recovery.

10

The Therapist
RESPONDING TO ROLE PROBLEMS

The personality disorder traits often observed among the addicted foster denial, externalization, blaming, and lack of self-knowledge. I have explained the need for the strong confrontation of group therapy, as opposed to weaker methods such as individual therapy, to overcome this denial and externalization. But you must also be aware that the addict is different from many people who seek psychotherapy. Nonaddicts seeking psychotherapy often realize that something is "wrong inside"; consequently, they quickly form a good working alliance with the therapist, searching for self-knowledge and self-improvement. This alliance is used to "fight" whatever symptoms or problems they are experiencing. Furthermore, they often feel enlightened and "freed" by the insights provided from therapy and are very appreciative of therapy and the therapist. They will often show their appreciation openly.

The addict more often has a defensive posture regarding therapy and in fact is "fighting" the therapist at first. The addict prefers to see problems as being something "outside" himself. He feels very uncomfortable and distressed when the therapist or group points out that he is both the architect and victim of his own addiction. The addict is not always appreciative of the therapist's efforts to help him see himself more clearly. He often expresses his anger and resentment openly to the therapist. He may attack the therapist and the group as a way of trying to defend against further revelations about himself.

The therapist may feel that he is desperately struggling to help this client and gain his confidence. He can easily become exhausted by the constant work of fighting the addict's defenses, especially when all this effort seems unappreciated. It is easy for the therapist to become disillusioned at this point, thinking that the client is really unmotivated. He may even begin to think, "Why not give up on this client?"

Here are several guidelines for the therapist to follow in approaching this problem:

DON'T STRUGGLE WITH PATHOLOGY

Struggling with pathology is futile. Instead, concentrate on doing your job the best you can. Provide the addict with accurate information about what is happening to him and how to respond to his addictive problem. When we begin to want more than this, we get ourselves into trouble. When we begin to yearn for the client to get well, and if he senses it, he may begin to try to manipulate us according to his old patterns. Such a client could very easily exploit his pathology, refusing to get well just to frustrate the therapist. Even more important, when we desperately want others to get well, we begin to attend too much to the outcome of therapeutic interventions and may easily delude ourselves into believing we can control those outcomes. This inevitably results in even more frustration, because we simply cannot control the outcome of therapy, nor how the client behaves. What we can control is our delivery of information and feedback to the client about what is happening and what he can do about it.

We must continue to give each client a choice as to how to live his life, refusing to enter a power struggle with him or demanding that the client "get well." Therapists working with addicts must realize that the client has the choice to become self-constructive or remain self-destructive. His decision is not something we have to change, it is something the client has to act upon. We can be more therapeutic and objective if we merely inform a client of the consequences of his behavior, without getting into a struggle to change it. This does not mean that we cannot develop and show real, genuine caring for the client. It just means that we must monitor our level of caring and keep it within a safe range, so that it doesn't jeopardize our ability to be honest with the client nor make us vulnerable to depression if he relapses.

Complicated, multidimensional relationships between a therapist and a client inevitably impede growth and recovery from addiction. A therapist should cultivate one, and only one, relationship with clients. That relationship is therapeutic. Becoming the client's confidant, friend, lover, partner in business, or pursuing any other form of business or personal relationship with the client is detrimental because it diverts the therapeutic focus; it is also highly unethical. If, for instance, a client agrees to reroof your house (even though you pay him), and does this while you are treating him, then you are somewhat obligated to him. This obligation complicates the therapeutic relationship with whatever other messages or transactions are generated by the additional interactions.

USE THE POWER OF THE GROUP

The group therapist's skills determine how stressed he will become to a great extent. The more we hone the group to confront and deal with problems, and genuinely give them this mission, the more powerful will be the interventions, the more change we are likely to see, and the less we, as individual change agents, will feel the need to personally encourage major changes in others.

If the therapist is relatively new and/or immature, there is a danger that he will often feel the need to "do something" to personally encourage major changes in others instead of empowering the group to deal with problems. As a result, this therapist may interfere far too much in group therapy and essentially become an authoritarian group leader, constantly dominating feedback, pressuring to lead and guide the group, and making crucial group decisions himself. From the perspective of the Friendly Forces model presented here, this therapist is working overtime, stressing himself by taking on so many of the group's responsibilities. By assuming such a strong role in the group, he overshadows the group, which then never becomes a powerful force for change. The group itself is now ineffectual and the therapist feels even more pressure to perform. The therapist experiences greater personal stress and the group becomes even weaker.

A more mature therapist knows that often "doing nothing" except monitoring the group process is definitely "doing something." By simply monitoring the group process instead of controlling the group's messages and interactions we give the group responsibility for its own growth and create a powerful feedback mechanism in support of client recovery. How does one develop this more mature attitude? I recommend that the therapists in a treatment facility discuss frequently the question, "What is our responsibility?" and that team members seriously think and rethink their position in the group.

Often, one of the reasons that a therapist assumes too much responsibility in a group is that he has a history of being the caretaker in his own family. When there was a problem, he moved in, took over, and solved the problem. In fact, this is often the history of professional caretakers such as physicians, social workers, psychologists, and counselors. When such persons become professionals, they often continue this earlier role of "moving in and taking over." One approach to dealing with this problem is to talk with other therapists about it and receive their feedback. Often, as with our clients, other staff can see when we're satisfying our own needs instead of the clients' and can enlighten us with their insights. Whenever we think any situation in the group requires a possible intervention, it is helpful to ask ourselves: "Who is responsible here for developing the group further? Is the group really hopelessly stuck? Am I absolutely sure that they need my interventions?" If we use this strategy and "take our own medicine," receiving feedback ourselves from other therapists and team members, then we have made a major move toward helping the group to develop maximum power, while avoiding unnecessary stress and "burnout" ourselves.

BUILD A STRONG TEAM

Strong teamwork is essential because of the resistive and often struggling nature of the client. Clients in the group will often verbally attack a therapist; at this time, it is very important to have a well-functioning team which can shift the focus back onto the group process:

[An open group discussion is taking place]

[Mr. C.]: I'd like to comment on the lunch room staff also. The other day, I asked politely for another serving of potatoes and the cook glared at me and said: 'Don't you know I've been cooking all morning and you've already eaten all the damn things.' I was tempted to haul off and knock hell out of the cook. But I just walked off. I think you should train your staff here— they're just not professional.

[Therapist 1]: Well, did you try to be assertive with the cook and tell him later how the interaction made you feel?

[Mr. C.]: Aw, don't go giving me that guff. You always want us to be assertive—I saw you the other day in group, you weren't assertive at all when Bernie [another group member] jumped all over you.

[Short uncomfortable silence]

[Therapist 2]: But Mr. C___, we're dealing with your feelings here, not the staff's feelings. What can you do to learn to handle these situations? You're going to face situations just like this once you are out of the hospital. And we won't be there to handle them for you—so, you have to learn to handle these sorts of situations for yourself. Let's talk about how you're handling the situation, instead of how the therapist is doing.

Later, the same teamwork can lead to a good post-processing of what happened, how it might have been handled better, a reaffirmation of the confrontation involved, and support for the clinician who may be experiencing self-doubt. It can become pretty lonesome when an aggressive group confronts you as a therapist, so consider how this can be handled well ahead of time.

Addicts may also try to split the team apart by consulting one, then another, member in an attempt to have their demands met and avoid facing their problems:

[Group counselor is walking down the corridor]

[Mr. G.]: Hey, doc, is it alright if I go over to the drugstore and get some of the coffee the guys were needing? I just discussed it with Nurse Picklee and she said it was alright, and she told me I should go ahead.

[Counselor]: Well, I guess it's okay.

[Later, counselor sees social worker]

[Counselor]: Damn, you know I saw Mr. G___ in the corridor and he told me that Nurse Picklee had told him he could go to the drugstore to get some coffee for the clients. I've repeatedly told her to check with me before she allows the clients to leave the hospital while program activities are taking place.

[Soc. Wkr.]: Maybe you'd better talk with her again.

[Counselor meets with Ms. Picklee]

[Counselor]:   You know, I met Mr. G____ in the corridor and he told me that you had told him it was okay to go to the drugstore for coffee even though he's supposed to be in his group now.

[Nurse]:   Good grief, he did tell me they were out of coffee and I told him later that he might ask you if he could go to the drugstore. But I pointedly told him that he could not go without getting your permission. He knew that very well. I believe we need to confront him about manipulating and conning the staff to get what he wants. This isn't the first time he's done this to avoid being confronted in group therapy.

This is an example of how clients sometimes try to manipulate and cause dissension among staff. These manipulations are particularly disruptive if there is low staff morale. Good communication and teamwork reduce the likelihood and impact of these routine problems.

The "burnout" syndrome. Another problem which disrupts staff cohesion and teamwork is the widely lamented burnout syndrome among addiction treatment professionals. It is termed burnout when a staff member who was enthusiastic and hopeful about the treatment of addicts becomes disillusioned and bitter, sometimes becoming moralistic, judgmental, and critical of addicts and their unsuccessful attempts at sobriety. Such burnt-out staff members will appear depressed, uttering statements like, "I can't stand my job any longer," or "I hate working with addicts now." Oddly enough, in my experience, these individuals rarely seek another job, demonstrating a kind of morbid dependency upon their work in this stage of their lives.

Staff burnout has an extremely damaging effect on a treatment program. It is virtually impossible for the group members not to feel the hopelessness such a burnt-out counselor feels about their future. Addicts are a population of people who have often become hopeless about their future and themselves, and desperately need someone to instill hope into their lives and believe that they can recover. In the more pathological situations, the counselors who develop severe burnout will actually begin to deal with clients in a very antitherapeutic way. They may demean the clients, being openly judgmental and critical, cold, and sarcastic. Although they may not be charged with client abuse in their facility, still, their tone and expression leave no doubt about what they think of the addict and his future.

Here, a frank discussion of staff attitudes and some problem solving about what to do is the first step. For example, it may be that the person who is burnt out needs to find another job or place of employment, perhaps in an entirely different field. In other situations, it may be possible for the burnt-out therapist to work on his attitudes toward addicts and to make some adjustments. The burnt-out counselor may be expecting too much of the addicts, much in excess of what is realistic. In other cases, the counselor may be unhappy with his personal life and may be taking it out on the addict, since the addict is in a weak and defenseless position. The addict always makes for a good "scapegoat"; we have often seen the families of addicts scapegoat the client, attributing all problems to him. If informal discussions and problem solving do not bring change, professional counseling of the burnt-out therapist may be recommended.

RESPONSIBILITY FOR OUTCOMES

I feel personally that it is a terrible mistake for the therapist to find satisfaction in the measure of progress a group makes. Instead, I recommend concentrating on following what our model tells us is the appropriate therapeutic approach and to develop internal pride in "doing what we are supposed to do." This is akin to the surgeon feeling good about performing an intricate operation perfectly even though the client eventually dies, for instance, in the case of a difficult and risky organ transplant. It is an approach which takes work and time to integrate into one's self. In essence, we have to learn to feel good about doing what we judge to be therapeutic, even though it does not always have a positive, short-term outcome.

The Friendly Forces model requires that the therapist be willing to relinquish some control over the short-term outcomes of the group therapy. I have advocated a place on the structural continuum, from "no structure" to "complete structure," which I think best suits group therapy with addicts. Having made this commitment, I must accept the short-term outcomes of the approach. Although I want each group to make fast and enduring progress toward self-knowledge and recovery, a particular group may seem to be unable to do this within the structural level of the model I've selected. In this case, it is better to let them struggle with the task at hand than to move up the continuum to more structure, or to discontinue group therapy. For example, a group might persist in asking questions. In response, I note that it is good for them to learn the fruitlessness of such questioning, even though I'm disturbed that the group doesn't seem to be making much progress in other areas. I must accept that some groups will stall, while others will take their task very far, and that it is not within my power as a therapist to completely control which outcome occurs.

These remarks are true for any therapy model or client population, but they are especially relevant to groups of character disordered persons, or persons with character disordered traits. These clients seem to provoke a desire within us to provide the internal controls they lack and to ultimately superimpose our entire perspective onto them.

PREDICTING CLIENT SUCCESS

Similarly, I would like to emphasize how difficult it is to predict who will ultimately succeed in a rehabilitation program. Even though there are general predictors which work when applied to group statistics, they often fail us when applied to individuals. I recall one case in particular, a man who returned to treatment again and again, a man the staff had given up on and joked about. Nevertheless, one day this individual decided to become sober and has stayed sober several years now, even taking a lead in chairing the A.A. meeting in one of the local hospitals! Everyone who works in a treatment center knows countless stories like this, cases where hope was lost, but change occurred.

Because we cannot accurately predict who will ultimately be successful in recovery, we must suspend judgment and concentrate upon performing what we believe is the appropriate therapeutic intervention. This is not to say that we shouldn't have empirical studies to see who gets better and who doesn't, or what the relevant factors are. It is simply that we must counteract our sometimes frantic concern for successful "outcome ratios" and our subsequent frustration when the results seem poor in the short term. If we attend primarily to what we should be doing therapeutically and feel good about doing our job, we can continue to offer services which will ultimately help many clients. From another perspective we must congratulate ourselves, sometimes with the quiet inner knowledge of having performed well, even when others, and perhaps the clients themselves, do not realize this.

This approach has secondary benefits in that, by becoming more self-reinforcing, the therapist is less dependent upon the client. This places him in an ideal position to confront the client objectively and to handle the often highly charged anger that results from the confrontation. Therapists who want to please clients or are too dependent upon the clients cannot be forthright with them and cannot handle their anger objectively. Client-dependent therapists who have not had their dependency needs met may be too harsh and critical in their feedback and hence, clients will dismiss it as "personal and emotional."

In summary, there are effective responses to the common stresses that addiction counselors face. The addiction counselor often faces an angry, defensive group of clients, ready to attack anyone to get the focus off themselves. It is here that the addiction counselor needs the secure support of the professional team. Further, persons with character disorder traits are not apt to return to treatment agents unless they are still in difficulty. This provides a biased, overly negative picture of the proportion of clients who are doing well. It is sometimes easy for the counselor who is attentive to immediate outcome data to become discouraged by relapsing clients and the chronic nature of addiction. In order to buffer oneself against such biased experiences, one must attend to performing therapeutically and let that be the measure of success. This is of course in lieu of having realistic data about the real rate of recovery from one's program. Unfortunately, most programs do not have the resources to gather complete and accurate data on long-term recovery rates. Survey methods usually render very few returns from the program graduates; these returns are sometimes highly biased, e.g. everyone who responds is sober.

11

A Brief Review
OF PRINCIPLES AND GUIDELINES

Group therapy is a psychological treatment for addiction, intended to increase an addict's understanding of self by revealing and clarifying the motivations, fears, and irrational ideas hidden behind dysfunctional behaviors. This awakening or sensitizing of the addict to inner realities occurs primarily through feedback from other addicts comprising "the group." We have seen that it is the addict's tremendous denial which prompts the use of group therapy to strongly augment and interpret the everyday reactions his behavior triggers. Through group therapy, we hope that the addict can become more analytic and rational about what is happening to him and how he is contributing to his problems.

The Friendly Forces model for group therapy creates groups of addicts who can give each other powerful feedback, moving collectively toward greater individual self-knowledge. Activating a group begins with getting acquainted and an orientation of members to each other and to the Friendly Forces model. We use some ice breakers to get members acquainted with each other and then gradually increase their intimacy through appropriate exercises and through a discussion of trust and confidentiality. An explanation of the Friendly Forces model includes information about how to make a presentation, stressing the emotional content of what has happened during the various stages of one's life.

The power of the group therapy model for addicts derives in part from one of the addict's characteristic strengths: *outsight*, an ability to be aware of and analytical about the feelings, motives, and behaviors of others. This is in sharp contrast to the addict's lack of *insight* concerning himself. Through group therapy, outsight and insight begin to converge.

I would like to reemphasize that the Friendly Forces model is not represented as being superior to other models of group therapy from a scientific viewpoint. It is a model or approach that, from my clinical perspective, produces efficient and effective therapy. It has worked for me. Also, while this approach is appropriate for character disordered clients whose reality contact is intact and who have no more than mild organic brain dysfunction, it is *inappropriate* for addicts who are psychotic or suffering from significant brain damage.

In *Conducting Group Therapy with Addicts*, I have described addiction as a multifaceted problem, one wherein genetic, social, and psychological forces influence the addict's choice to repeatedly use chemical substances as a major coping device. I have explained how, in the development of an addict's personality, there is a gradual shifting of focus to the "outer environment," with an accompanying neglect of the development of inner resources. We have seen that this shift to a virtually exclusive preoccupation with externals leads to the addict's often-observed characteristics of:

- demandingness;
- blaming;
- obsession with manipulation and control of others and oneself;
- preoccupation with personal power;
- reliance upon acting out (including major uses of drugs/alcohol as acting out behaviors); and,
- denial.

In group therapy, these tendencies are revealed in an addict's presentations. "Outsightful" group members, themselves addicts, detect these tendencies in personal accounts or presentations, reflecting them back to the presenter for him to acknowledge and deal with. The reflecting back of these outsights by group members is termed feedback. It is feedback which contains the messages of group therapy. Therefore, a crucial task for the therapist is to guide feedback so that it is both powerful and therapeutic. Therapists should follow these essential rules in conducting group therapy with addicts:

- Focus on one client per session.
- Emphasize the personal history and internal feelings in an attempt to gain self-awareness.
- Encourage direct and honest feedback.

Crystal clear outsight on the part of group members doesn't always translate into effective feedback. There are simple techniques, however, which amplify feedback and which can be readily explained and demonstrated to group members:

- Maintain eye contact.
- Address the presenter directly.
- Make statements instead of asking questions.
- Use assertiveness in the feedback process.
- Avoid moralizing.
- Focus on what is happening rather than giving advice.
- Include one's emotional reactions in the feedback statements.
- Help the group members face responsibility rather than "rescuing" them.

Therapists encounter several common problems during group therapy presentations by addicts. These were illustrated, along with suggestions for what can be done to correct them:

- premature presentations;
- overly factual presentations or drunkalogues; and,
- brief presentations.

Likewise, there are problems which are commonly encountered by the therapist during feedback. These behaviors have an adverse effect upon the outcomes of group therapy and must be arrested or reshaped:

- rescuing;
- failing to give feedback;
- hostile or aggressive feedback; and,
- indirect feedback.

The therapist, either individually or as part of a professional team, establishes guidelines for the group process and intervenes to redirect it when it is absolutely essential to do so. To develop the group's capability, responsibility, and authority, I recommend that the therapist adopt a management style which:

- places maximum responsibility on the group for self-management and outcomes;
- fades from the process as much as the group will allow, increasing the group's responsibility;
- recognizes that the power of the group inheres in the group and that every intervention should be guided by this principle in order to enhance that power;
- keeps "hands off" so long as the group is progressing;
- intervenes in such a way as to reduce the need for further interventions if possible;
- avoids any unnecessary interpretations of behavior;
- encourages all members to give feedback; and,
- gives the group feedback about how it is functioning, if necessary.

A critical aspect of managing group therapy is observing and assessing the group's status and progress. Some important clues a therapist can use to assess group progress were explained and illustrated:

- body language and general "feel" of the group;
- the emotional climate;
- the behavior of the group members;
- the energy level of the group; and,
- the cohesion in the group.

The therapist can expect to encounter some typical process problems. I have described how these problems typically evolve and what to do when they happen in your group:

- failure to recognize or deal with process or group cohesion problems;
- disruptive overprocessing; and,
- excessive focus on externals.

A team approach is recommended for group therapy with addicts because it helps keep the process centered on the group during externalizing attacks on the therapist—a highly disruptive group process problem. Ideally, the professional group therapy team would be multidisciplinary, a structure which promotes the discussion of client and group dynamics from many different professional perspectives: medical, social work, nursing, psychiatric, and psychological.

The basic stages of group therapy—beginning, middle and transition-to-aftercare—were discussed, with emphasis upon the middle stage. It is here that the group generally "takes off," achieving a high degree of cohesion; or "gets stuck" in low efficiency and productivity. Various approaches to solving group problems were discussed, particularly the "open group" discussion with its focus upon highlighting and seeking solutions for obvious group problems.

Finally, I have covered some of the considerations in helping therapists maintain their enthusiasm and efficiency in dealing continually with the resistance and denial so typical of the addict. Several guidelines for dealing with these stressful situations were given, including:

- learning to simply perform our responsibility and let the addict be responsible for his part of the therapy, without getting into power struggles with the addict;
- utilizing the power of the group, instead of trying to use our own personal and very limited power over the addict;
- building a strong team effort to support and assist each other, as well as using such teams for personal feedback as it relates to performance of therapeutic responsibilities;
- accepting the outcome of the model chosen as well as its limitations; and,
- learning to reinforce ourselves for carrying out our responsibilities so that we can let the clients be responsible for themselves.

I hope this book is helpful to practicing therapists and students who are facing the challenge of working with addicts. Good luck with the challenge of providing quality group therapy!

Selected Bibliography

Printed Materials

Alcoholics Anonymous World Services, Inc. *Alcoholics Anonymous*. New York: Alcoholics Anonymous World Services, Inc., 1976.

American Psychiatric Association. *Diagnostic and Statistical Manual of Mental Disorders. 3rd ed., revised.* Washington: American Psychiatric Association, 1987.

Armor, David J., J. Michael Polich, and Harriet B. Stambul. *Alcoholism and Treatment*. New York: John Wiley and Sons, 1978.

Barry, Herbert, III. "Psychological Factors in Alcoholism." In *The Biology of Alcoholism*, Vol. III, eds. Benjamin Kissin and Henri Begleiter. New York: Plenum, 1974.

Beardslee, William R. and George E. Vaillant. "Prospective Prediction of Alcoholism and Psychopathology." *Journal of Studies on Alcohol* 45 (1984): 500-503.

Carson, Robert C., James N. Butcher, and James C. Coleman. *Abnormal Psychology and Modern Life*. Glenview, Illinois: Scott, Foresman and Company, 1988.

Williams, Allan F. "The Alcoholic Personality." In *The Biology of Alcoholism, Vol. IV*, eds. Benjamin Kissin and Henri Begleiter. New York: Plenum, 1976.

Videos

Elder, Ivan. *A Client Orientation to Group Psychotherapy*. Bradenton: FL: Human Services Institute, 1990.